McLuhan

FOR BEGINNERS™

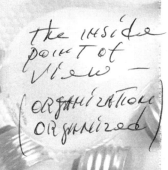

the inside
point of
view —
(ORGANIZATION
ORGANIZED)

medium,
the power
of its
effect.

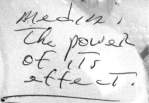

Something
Indispensible
cannot do
without.

WRITERS AND READERS PUBLISHING, INC.
P.O. Box 461, Village Station
New York, NY 10014

Writers and Readers Limited
9 Cynthia Street
London N1 9JF
England

•

Text Copyright: © 1997, W. Terrence Gordon
Illustrations © 1997, Susan Willmarth
Cover & Book Design: Terrie Dunkelberger

A Writers and Readers Documentary Comic Book
Copyright © 1997
ISBN # 0-86316- Trade 231-2
1 2 3 4 5 6 7 8 9 0

Manufactured in the United States of America

"Archimedes once said, 'Give me a place to stand and I will move the world.' Today he would have pointed to our electric media and said, 'I will stand on your eyes, your ears, your nerves, and your brain, and the world will move in any tempo or pattern I choose'"

-Marshall McLuhan
Understanding Media, page 68.

CONTENTS

ACKNOWLEDGMENTS

The author gratefully acknowledges the help of the following people:

Eric McLuhan

Arthur Kroker

Greg Skinner

John Barry

Lee Robertson

Jane Williamson

and Tim, isn't this a surprise,

after all these years?

McLuhan

FOR BEGINNERS ™

WRITTEN BY W. TERRENCE GORDON
ILLUSTRATED BY SUSAN WILLMARTH

Writers and Readers

f you are like most people, you've probably heard of Marshall McLuhan—the man *Playboy* magazine called "the High Priest of Popcult" and the "Metaphysician of Media"—and you probably even recognize a couple of the phrases he came up with—*"the medium is the message"* and *"the global village"*—but that's about it. Not only have you never read any of McLuhan's books, you've probably never read anything that makes you think you should.

I have news for you: McLuhan may be the most under-rated thinker of our time. But don't take my word for it. Here's what others have said:

BRITISH CRITIC GEORGE STEINER

"He has joyously enriched the scope of what is relevant. He has made the jungle of the world more interesting."

AMERICAN CRITIC GERALD STEARN

"He can only be considered a stimulating thinker on a scale quite similar to Freud and Einstein."

NEWSWEEK MAGAZINE

"...[McLuhan's theory of communication offers nothing less than an explanation of all human culture, past, present and future. And he excites large passions."

Newsweek

MARCH 6, 1967   40¢

The Message of Marshall McLuhan

"...the new environment that McLuhan discerns should be studied as carefully as the O_2 system in the Apollo spaceship. Just possibly, understanding McLuhan may help ensure that earth's environment sustains rather than destroys the crew."

"McLuhan is a synthesizer. He has gathered amorphous and scattered ideas, thought them through with force and vivaci-ty, and opened up new areas of awareness."

"McLuhan's teaching is radical, new, animated by high intelligence, and capable of moving people to social action. If he is wrong, it matters."

"Suppose he *is* what he sounds like, the most important thinker since Newton, Darwin, Freud, Einstein, and Pavlov...*what if he is right?*"

the Important Thinkers

McLuhan was an obscure Canadian professor of English till he published *Understanding Media: The Extensions of Man* in 1964. The paperback edition became the fastest selling nonfiction book at Harvard and other universities—with no advertising or promotion! *Understanding Media* was the book that brought Marshall McLuhan to public attention as a media analyst and catapulted him to international prominence. For the next fifteen years, McLuhan lectured passionately to academic *and* popular audiences, engaging in all kinds of debates and forums around the world on his key theme: how technology affects the forms and scale of social organization and individual lives.

Understanding Media:
The Extensions of Man
Marshall McLuhan
with a new Introduction and Bibliography by the Author.
$1.95
McGraw-Hill Paperbacks

By 1980, the year McLuhan died, cable TV had not yet come to the Amazon jungle. The inhabitants of the "global village" he spoke of still knew nothing, or little, about inter-active television, PCs, CDs, talking books, the World Wide Web, termi-nal node controllers, optical discs, pocket computers, the Internet, optical fiber or laser technology.

But it is McLuhan's work that provided a framework to let us study and understand all these media.

BUT THAT WAS THEN. WHAT ABOUT NOW?

A few years ago, when *Wired*, the terminally hip, "future-friendly," magazine of the computer age was hyperconceived, Marshall McLuhan was chosen as the magazine's "patron saint." *Wired* exploded into 1996 by featuring McLuhan in their January issue. Three articles and a handsome, spare-no-expense cover were supposed to be a tribute to McLuhan. (His ghost thanks you.) Unfortunately, the *Wired* articles so drastically misrepresented his teaching that many readers must have wondered: why bother with McLuhan?—there's nothing to be gained from <u>reading</u> him.

Gee Thanks

(It was McLuhan who quipped "Unless a statement is startling, no one will pay any attention; they will put it down as a point of view.") But it is probably McLuhan's wide-ranging thought that has revived his reputation among the Net-surfers and Web-crawlers of the 1990s:

With all due respect to the cyberspace cadets at *Wired*, Marshall McLuhan's books—especially his seminal works, *The Mechanical Bride* (1951), *The Gutenberg Galaxy: The Making of Typographic Man* (1962), *Understanding Media* (1964), *Through the Vanishing Point* (with Harley Parker, 1968), *From Cliché to Archetype* (with Wilfred Watson, 1970), *Laws of Media: The New Science* (with Eric McLuhan, 1988)—are enough to rank him among the most brilliant, creative and challenging thinkers of the twentieth century. And he was enough of a showman to be interesting!

Mark Dery, writing in *Educom Review* (November/December 1995):

"McLuhan's ideas cast a powerful spell on fringe computer culture, where they have acquired a New Age aura...McLuhan's unexpected resurrection, just in time for the new millennium, finds him in a strange new incarnation...the first theologian of information" (p. 28).

Lewis Lapham, in the Introduction to MIT Press's thirtieth-anniversary reissue of <u>Understanding Media</u>:

"Seldom in living memory had so obscure a scholar descended so abruptly from so remote a garret into the center ring of the celebrity circus, but McLuhan accepted the transformation as if it were nothing out of the ordinary..."

"Much of what McLuhan had to say makes a good deal more sense in 1994 than it did in 1964."

"...the events of the last thirty years have proved him more often right than wrong."

All this, and still the Republican Speaker of the House, Newt Gingrich, recently counted (or discounted) McLuhan among the lowest of the low, calling him a "countercultural McGovernik."

—HEY, WAS MCLUHAN WAYYYY AHEAD OF HIS TIME, OR WHAT!?!

*B*efore we get into McLuhan's life story, it will be helpful to briefly describe his rather unique point of view...

McLuhan's Point of View—

> IN A WORD: HE DIDN'T HAVE ONE.

S·O·R·T OF

McLuhan's approach to any question was to refuse to have a fixed viewpoint. For McLuhan, understanding always requires a multidimensional approach. To fully understand anything, he argued, you have to look at it from several points of view. So, McLuhan would have gone against his own beliefs and teaching with just a single take on anything. With no fixed viewpoint, his writings present no complex argument, no thesis developed over a long stretch.

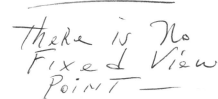

11

In the preface to his first book, *The Mechanical Bride*, an incisive study of the effects of magazine advertising and comics, McLuhan says there is no need to read the chapters in order. That was the way he <u>wanted</u> it!

—Readers were freed from relying on the linear structure of conventional books!—

The unsettling result in *The Mechanical Bride* was intended. McLuhan claimed that his work offered a mosaic, or field, approach to the questions he studied, in the same way that the media effects he probed reorganized audiences' perceptions of the world around them (more on "probes" later). In *The Gutenberg Galaxy*, McLuhan jolts his readers into an awareness of how books function as a medium (more on this later, too!)

The point is, if we read *The Gutenberg Galaxy* or other books by McLuhan with the discomfitting feeling that we have not read such works before, and ask ourselves what makes McLuhan's books different, then we get a starting point for some pretty astounding insights into what media and their real messages are all about.

But McLuhan also warned that such reorganization of perception could be bewildering to those who cling to the older, linear order of things and a single "practical" point of view.

He cautioned that we should step into his writings the way we step into a bath:

—The exact entry point is of no importance, because a moment later we will be in a new environment—

...*water in the case of the bath,*
...*media in the case of McLuhan.*

$\mathcal{S}$o, the organization of a McLuhan book is more like that of a newspaper. Yet, while stepping <u>into</u> a newspaper is inevitable, McLuhan claimed that stepping <u>back</u> from it, to perceive it as an <u>environment</u>, is indispensable to understanding its power and its effect.

Continued from Page B13

criticize me for sitting. I won't waver from my decision."

Abdul-Rauf, who is in the second year of a four-year, $11.2 million contract, stands to lose $31,707 for every game he misses, $665,853 if he does not return this season.

Keith Glass, a New Jersey agent who represents Abdul-Rauf, said: "I don't think Mahmoud will stand for the anthem. Whether I, you, or someone else likes it is not the issue. Clearly, he's been damaged. Not just financially, but his reputation, as well. And it's going to haunt him until people understand how he's feeling."

According to a lawyer for the union, the league suspended Abdul-Rauf without first notifying the players association. At one point, several people with knowledge of the case said Abdul-Rauf was given the option of either staying in the dressing room or walkway during the national anthem. That is no longer an option for his return, a basketball official said yesterday.

In his statement yesterday, which was read by his representative,

... his feelings about the anthem.

"I am also a man who tries to perfect my life on and off the court, and someone who tries to be sincere in my treatment of my fellow human beings, and sincere," he said. "Therefore, it is my understanding, and sincerity is therefore, it is my understanding and sincerity in participation. As such I cannot in participation ... national anthem ... to disrespect ... or half ... the locker ... was being ... while the anth ... Abdul-Rau ... In some cas ... gaged in stretching exerci ... near the court ... mise can be ... could wind up in ... Amendment like ...

Martin Garbus, ... ney and First Am ... said: "The First Am ... applies against the government ... doesn't apply to private entities. The question becomes: Is the N.B.A. sufficiently public that the First Amendment should apply? It is a relatively new question, a very profound question."

Garbus added: "There is a difference between religious and political belief..."

years at Louisiana St before turning pro.

He suffers from ... drome, a genetic dis ... manifests itself in it ... This s ... the league ... point ... Among Mu ... Koran specifi ... the ... However, ... associated ... secretary of ... society of Noi ... sion at wh ... anthem and ... own conscie ... In Denv ... Abdul-Rau ... side of the ... asked ... self is ... attorney, ... is one ... Nuggets' leading ... each. ... scorer who turned 27 years old ... was born Chris Jackson in ... red as schoolboy player in ... Gulfport, Miss., and then for two ...

106
82

to have that free-ball."
'm the type of play-
ot real quick, run off
, then miss a couple
right back on. As a
ave to have that free-
st has to roll with you.
d with me."
aste for Minnesota was
h 23 points from the
m Kevin Garnett, who
ls, blocked 2 shots and
ds.
Nelson Knicks, mean-
to 10 games over .500
ating Minnesota (19-43)
it shooting and 4 fewer
n their 45. They played
Patrick Ewing, who

TENNIS

Marques night,
sociated Press

"The inside point of view would coincide with the practical point of view of the man who would rather eat the turtle than admire the design on its back. The same man would rather dunk himself in the newspaper than have any esthetic or intellectual grasp of its character and meaning." (*The Mechanical Bride*, p. 4)

$\mathcal{L}$et us now step into McLuhan's biography. Who was Marshall McLuhan and how did he come to be called the sage of the television age?

Stepping

Into

McLuhan

I hate T.V. & will not own an E-mail address

Before he was the subject of an off-Broadway play*, before he played himself in Woody Allen's *Annie Hall*, before he gave the world eyes and ears for what it is to have eyes and ears in *Understanding Media*, Marshall McLuhan was a professor of English who loved James Joyce, hated television, denounced "Dagwood," and explained all three. Even though he is the hero of a new generation of cybernauts and Information Highway trekkies, if McLuhan were alive today, he would probably refuse to have an e-mail address!

> *BUT HE WOULD WANT TO CONTINUE FIRING OFF IDEAS, MACHINE-GUN STYLE, IN HIS MONDAY NIGHT MEDIA SEMINARS AT THE UNIVERSITY OF TORONTO'S CENTER FOR CULTURE AND TECHNOLOGY.*

* "The Medium" played to enthusiastic audiences at the New York Theater Workshop in 1993-94 and earned actor Tom Nelis an Obie award for his portrayal of McLuhan.

DON'T PICTURE A SPRAWLING BUNKER OF GLASS AND CONCRETE OR A SOARING TOWER HERE— THIS WAS LITERALLY A ONE-HORSE OPERATION: A CONVERTED, TURN-OF-THE-CENTURY COACH HOUSE TUCKED AWAY BEHIND AN OLD MANSION ON THE UNIVERSITY OF TORONTO'S DOWNTOWN CAMPUS.

McLuhan launched the Center in 1964 but had to jam his collaborators and students into his tiny office for four years before "moving up" to the coach house! At least the coach—and horse—were long since gone.

And he would want to continue infuriating a world moving into the twenty-first century with nineteenth century perceptions. And he would—oh, right, back to the biography...

Marshall McLuhan was born in 1911 in Edmonton, Canada, and raised in Winnipeg. He received his B.A. (1933) and M.A. (1934) from the University of Manitoba, earning a second B.A. in English literature from Cambridge University (England) in 1936. The lessons McLuhan learned during those early days at Cambridge formed the base for his later studies of media. Which brings us to the question: How did a Canadian professor of English become a world-renowned, avant-garde media guru?

ANSWER

CRANE

crane

CRANE

crane

By extending lessons on language learned from one of his own teachers—namely I. A. Richards, whose lectures McLuhan attended at Cambridge University in the 1930s. Richards pioneered an approach to literary criticism that focused on the meaning of words and how they are used. He deplored the "proper meaning superstition," the belief that word-meanings are fixed and independent of their use, and he forcefully illustrated the power of words to control thought.

?

Richards argued that thought should bring words under **its** control by determining meaning from context. This was the key idea of the book he wrote with C. K. Ogden, called *The Meaning of Meaning*. The idea stayed with McLuhan right through to his later writings.

> "All media are active metaphors in their power to translate experience into new forms. The spoken word was the first technology by which man was able to let go of his environment in order to grasp it in a new way." (<u>Understanding Media</u>, p. 57)

NEANDER-TECH
CAVE →

the Real thing...

Real?

?

Even more to the point is this example from 1972 with unmistakable echoes from Richards:

"Nothing has its meaning alone. Every figure [consciously noted element of a structure or situation] must have its ground or environment [the rest of the structure or situation which is not noticed]. A single word, divorced from its linguistic ground would be useless. A note in isolation is not music. Consciousness is corporate action involving all the senses (Latin sensus communis or 'common sense' is the translation of all the senses into each other). The 'meaning of meaning' is relationship."

(Take Today, p. 30)

Richards viewed any act of understanding or acquiring knowledge as a matter of interpreting and reinterpreting—a process he called "translation." A key chapter in McLuhan's *Understanding Media*, titled "Media as Translators," not only picks up this theme but links it to Richards's observations on the multiplicity of sensory channels:

" Our very word 'grasp' or 'apprehension' points to the process of getting at one thing through another, of handling and sensing many facets at a time through more than one sense at a time. It begins to be evident that 'touch' is not skin but the interplay of the senses, and 'keeping in touch' or 'getting in touch' is a matter of a fruitful meeting of the senses, of sight translated into sound and sound into movement, and taste and smell." (p. 60) "

Of course, there were many sources of influence on McLuhan's thought besides I. A. Richards, but few that came so early in his career or endured so long. Beyond Richards, the sources of influence on McLuhan were many and varied:

☞ **the French symbolist poets of the late 19th century**

☞ **the Irish writer James Joyce**

☞ **the English painter and writer Wyndham Lewis**

☞ **Anglo-American poet and critic T. S. Eliot**

☞ **American poet Ezra Pound**

☞ **literary critic F. R. Leavis**

☞ **Canadian economic historian Harold Innis.**

The richness of McLuhan's thought comes from the unique meshing of all these sources and the "feedforward" (another idea from I. A. Richards) he developed as a method for understanding popular culture and media.

Meanwhile Back at McLuhan's Bio...

During his first stint at Cambridge University, McLuhan converted to Roman Catholicism, under the influence of such writers as G. K. Chesterton, and was received into the church in Madison, Wisconsin in 1937. After one year of teaching at the University of Wisconsin, he moved to St. Louis University Though just twenty-five years old when he began his teaching career, McLuhan was shocked to find a "generation gap" between himself and his students. Feeling an urgent need to bridge this gap, he set out to understand what he suspected as its cause—the effect of mass media on American culture. He was on his way to writing his first book—*The Mechanical Bride* (1951).

McLuhan returned to Cambridge to work on a Ph. D. (completed in 1943) on the work of the sixteenth-century English pamphleteer and satirist Thomas Nashe. Coming home to Canada, he taught briefly at the University of Windsor (1944-46) before settling into a thirty-four-year-long career at the University of Toronto. Novelist Tom Wolfe, in a wonderfully wacky article on McLuhan, takes perverse pleasure in describing McLuhan at the height of his celebrity, ever the professor...

"He sits in a little office off on the edge of the University of Toronto that looks like the receiving bin of a second-hand book store, grading papers, _grading papers_, for days on end, wearing—well, he doesn't seem to care what he wears. If he feels like it, he just puts on the old striped tie with the plastic neck band. You just snap the plastic band around your neck and there the tie is, hanging down and ready to go..."
(In Gerald E. Stearn, ed., McLuhan Hot and Cool, p. 31)

McLuhan's earliest writings distinguished him as a fine literary critic, but in 1951, when he published <u>The Mechanical Bride</u> and tore a strip off advertising, popular culture, and comic strips, his long-standing interest in media became the focus of his books. Dropping his academic prose for a jazzier, more elliptical, and journalistic style, McLuhan began examining the pop objects of the emerging technological age.

Now if you are wondering what the title <u>The Mechanical Bride</u> means, McLuhan himself summed it up by saying that the book is about the death of sex.

THE DEATH OF SEX?!? WHO KILLED IT?

Madison Avenue did, with magazine advertising that gives everything from death to sex the same treatment and reduces humans to dreaming robots.

In 1953, McLuhan founded the Magazine _Explorations_ to publish works on language and media. In 1955, he formed a company called Idea Consultants. The outfit offered a creative business advice service and promoted some innovations of its own. These were not always big hits:

☺ a muffler attachment for using exhaust fumes to kill lawn rodents in their burrows

☺ lawnmower headlights (well, if you don't asphyxiate the little devils, you can take a crack at scaring them to death when they try to get some sleep)

☺ 3-D fireplaces

☺ airborne gift packages (promotional samples to be released by balloon)

Slightly better ideas that just never made it:

☺ the Peel-Aid (adhesive bandage on a tape-style dispenser)

☺ transparent training potties (to solve the lift-and-check problem)

And a lot of others that were well ahead of their time:

☺ aluminum soft drink containers

☺ cartons for alcoholic beverages

☺ electronic garage door openers

☺ frozen diet dinners

☺ toilet preparations in single-use disposable foil capsules

☺ "television platters" (videocassettes more than twenty years before they came on the market)

BLAH BLAHBLAH

FIRE WARNING

McLuhan's second book, *The Gutenberg Galaxy*, warned anyone who was looking that he was a seriously brilliant and totally unconventional man. *Galaxy* won him the Canadian Governor-General's Award for nonfiction in 1962 and established his reputation in the Western Hemisphere as a unique thinker.

Exploring the Gutenberg Galaxy

(Or: The Fifteenth Century According to Marshall McLuhan)

In the mid-fifteenth century, a German gent named Johannes Gutenberg invented movable type. This invention led to another—the printing press.

> WHAT SORT OF CHANGES DID THIS BRING OUT?

For McLuhan this is always the most important question, so let's find out what he had to say...

On the one hand, McLuhan explains, it meant the end of manuscript culture. But he also argued that the consequences were much more far-reaching than simply the loss of jobs for scribes and monks. Printing, he points out, led to the mechanization of writing, which led to the promotion of nationalism and national languages, because international Latin did not have enough scope to provide markets for all the printers.

By making books available to individual readers in such large numbers, the new print medium also fostered a sense of private identity and imposed a level of standardization in language that had not prevailed until then. So, "correct" spelling and grammar became a measure of literacy.

However, rather than diminish the effects of the older technology of writing, McLuhan suggests, print culture <u>intensified</u> it. Acording to McLuhan, before the invention of the alphabet, communication among humans involved all the senses simultaneously (speaking being accompanied by gestures and requiring both listening and looking). The immediacy and rich complexity of this type of communication was reduced by the alphabet to an abstract visual code.

"LOOK"
BEHIND YOU WITHOUT
TURNING AROUND

NOW YOU ARE IN
ACOUSTIC SPACE

before writing became widespread, McLuhan claims, humankind lived in acoustic space, the space of the spoken word. This space is boundless, directionless, horizonless, and charged with emotion. Writing transformed space into something bounded, linear, ordered, structured, and rational. The written page, with its edges, margins, and sharply defined letters in row after row brought about a new way of thinking about space.

McLuhan claimed that the portable book "was like a hydrogen bomb," from whose aftermath "a whole new environment—the Gutenberg Galaxy—emerges." His scenario goes something like this:

Space of the written word...

"Gutenberg's invention of movable type forced man to comprehend in a linear, uniform, connected, continuous fashion."

Then linear thought produced...

**"...economically...
the assembly line and
industrial society"**

**"...in physics...the Newtonian and
Cartesian views of the universe as a
mechanism in which it is possible to locate a
physical event in space and time"**

"...in art,...perspective"

"...in literature...the chronological narrative"

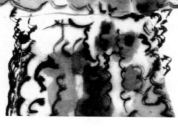

There is more—much more—in *The Gutenberg Galaxy* but it expands into and dovetails with the full bloom of McLuhan's vision in *Understanding Media*, so we'll put it on hold till we get there.

IN A NUTSHELL, MCLUHAN'S IDEA IS THAT THERE HAVE BEEN THREE AGES OF MAN:

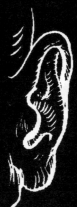

I.
The Preliterate or Tribal Era

—when the spoken word was king and the ear was queen—

II.
The Gutenberg Age

—when the printed word was king and the eye was queen—

III.
The Electronic Age of Retribalized (that's right!) Man

—when FULL sensory involvement (especially touching) is believing— when all the senses are jesters at the royal court—(and there is no king or queen)

Understanding

Understanding

Media

In this book McLuhan notes that his objective is not to offer a static theory of human communication but to <u>probe</u> the effects of anything humans use in dealing with the world. "To understand media," he wrote,

"ONE MUST PROBE EVERY-THING...INCLUDING THE WORDS... AND ONE'S SELF."

If that approach makes academics nervous, it is certainly one that every artist is comfortable with.

McLuhan's method? It's all in the fingers:

"Most of my work in the media is like that of a safecracker. In the beginning I don't know what's inside. I just set myself down in front of the problem and begin to work. I grope, I probe, I listen, I test—until the tumblers fall and I'm in." (From the Introduction to Gerald Stearn's <u>McLuhan</u> <u>Hot</u> <u>and</u> <u>Cool</u>)

the Probe

McLuhan called his way of thinking and investigating "probes" (you know, like the things we shot off into outer space in the '60s and '70s?) Throughout his writings he relies on such probes to gain insight into media and their effects.

To many academics of McLuhan's era, his concept of probes remains one of the most irritating aspects of his method. Faith in the power of the probe allowed McLuhan to take stabs at a wide range of topics, from the serious to the ridiculous, without necessarily committing himself to conclusions or testing his hypotheses scientifically—a habit that infuriated his critics and detractors.

TWO "PROBING" QUESTIONS

During McLuhan's heyday, people argued for hours about what he **really** meant. In Woody Allen's charming film "Annie Hall," Woody and Diane Keaton were standing in a movie line, when a nerd ahead of them started spouting off about what McLuhan **really** meant, McLuhan—who just happened to be standing nearby—began to explain himself. (Actually, to *misquote* himself.) One of McLuhan's favorite retorts to hecklers was "You think my fallacy is all wrong?" But in the film, McLuhan's "probing" question was changed into a statement: "You mean my fallacy is all wrong."

QUESTION: Why do you think McLuhan was displeased with the change he was asked to make in the form of this quip in his cameo as himself in "Annie Hall"?

Answer: In the film, McLuhan's question is turned into a statement and is no longer a disabling tactic against an aggressive opponent. As a question, it forces an opponent to stop and think, because it is unexpected—a probe! As a statement, it loses this force and undermines the authority that McLuhan represents in the scene.

Canadian artist Alan Flint shapes words out of wood, brick, cardboard, plastic, plaster, etc. In a field he dug out the word WOUND in giant letters to symbolize the effect of human systems on the earth.

QUESTION: Is this an example of the medium being the message?

Answer: Yes. For McLuhan, language is technology and words are artifacts. Flint's WOUND is part of the technology of language executed in a way that reminds us that the technology of digging *wounds* the earth. Flint weds his words to different technologies but in every case reminds us of the link between the word's meaning and the technology used in spelling it out. He also reminds us that words are artifacts and forces us to reflect on the medium and the message by forcing them together in new ways. (This is an example of an artist making probes out of clichés, a process that is explained in detail on page 107.)

YOU DON'T LIKE THOSE IDEAS? I GOT OTHERS.

And, boy, did he ever! <u>Wired</u> notes that while McLuhan was a political conservative and a devout Catholic, "his pronouncements on current events always add an element of loony dispassion and professional absent-mindedness" (January 1996, p.125) McLuhan was, to say the least, a *prolific* thinker. The following are just a few of his more clever responses to pop culture phenomena and whatever else snagged the attention of his rapid-fire mind. (We're not quoting him here—just summing up his takes on the subject-of-the-day.)

Time Magazine? Intellectual Pablum spooned out with all the cues for the right reaction.

Reader's Digest? It stimulates curiosity with its endless emphasis on making the impossible happen, cluttering the mind (a sort of cerebral **in**digestion) of readers who might otherwise feast on reading material of a greater intellectual challenge.

The twentieth century? The age that moved beyond invention to studying process (whether in literature, painting, or science) in isolation from product.

King Lear? The play is a model for the transition from the integrated world of roles to the fragmented world of jobs.

Schizophrenia? Perhaps an inevitable consequence of the sensory imbalance created by literacy.

MAD Magazine? mocks the hot media by replaying them cool

Renaissance Italy? Like a Hollywood assemblage of sets of antiquity.

Panic about automation? It is a reaction that perpetuates the dominant nineteenth century model of mechanical standardization and fragmentation of work.

Alice in Wonderland? Dislocated the concepts of time and space as uniform and continuous—concepts that had prevailed since the Renaissance.

The city? A collective extension of our skins.

Weapons? Extensions of hands, nails, and teeth.

Hitler? His demagoguery was ideally suited to radio, but if television had already been widespread in his day, he would have disappeared quickly.

Football? It is displacing baseball because it is non-positional, decentralized, and corporate—qualities of the electronic age.

The clock? It is a machine that turns out the uniform products of seconds, minutes and hours on an assembly-line pattern, separating time from the rhythm of human experience.

Earth-orbiting satellites? They put an end to nature by creating a new environment for the earth.

LUNCH BREAK QUIT

Strippers? They wear their audience when they take off their clothes. The audience creates a new environment (new clothing) for the stripper.

Violence? The creativity and the search for identity of the oppressed.

...but don't forget señor, education before action...

Women of the EZLN

The videophone? If it replaces the telephone, the world will become a global theater, with no boundaries between education, entertainment, and business.

The car following the horse? The car displaced the horse as transportation, but the horse made a comeback in the domain of entertainment and sport. Now that the car has been displaced by the jet, the car is taking on a new role as art and costume.

Hello?

The Journal of Irreproducible Results? It satirizes the specialist knowledge that belongs to the Gutenberg age.

John Maynard Keynes?
The great economist failed to take into account the consequences of the shift from monetary hardware (gold reserves) to monetary software (credit).

Karl Marx? The founder of communism failed to take into account the service environments that arise from the production of goods.

OOPS!

The internal combustion engine? It was the engine of change that integrated the society of whites and blacks in the U. S. South when private cars and trucks became available.

BUT HOLD IT, WE'RE PUTTING THE CART BEFORE THE HORSE (SOMETHING MCLUHAN HAD NO PROBLEM WITH, BY THE WAY), SO LET'S GET BACK TO MCLUHAN ON MEDIA AND THEIR EFFECTS.

When McLuhan first came to the attention of the general public in the 1960s, many assumed that he was promoting the end of book culture and embracing the age of television. In fact, he was cautioning that the then-new medium of television had enormous power. Publicly, he called it "the timid giant" and urged awareness of that power.

> PRIVATELY, HIS AVERSION TO THE TUBE WAS SO STRONG THAT HE PLEADED WITH HIS SON ERIC NOT TO LET THE GRANDCHILDREN WATCH TV!!

Lewis Lapham says that McLuhan's thinking about media begins with two premises: on the one hand, he notes, McLuhan argued that "we become what we behold;" on the other, he stated that "we shape our tools, and thereafter our tools shape us." McLuhan saw media as <u>make-happen</u> rather than <u>make-aware</u> agents, as systems more similar in nature to roads and canals than to objects of art or models of behavior.

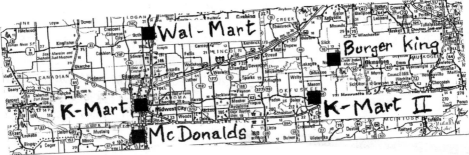

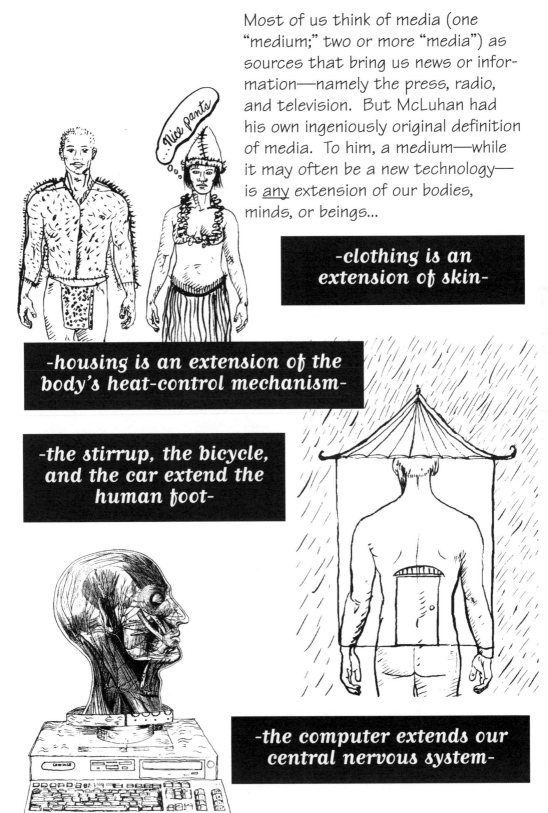

Most of us think of media (one "medium;" two or more "media") as sources that bring us news or information—namely the press, radio, and television. But McLuhan had his own ingeniously original definition of media. To him, a medium—while it may often be a new technology—is <u>any</u> extension of our bodies, minds, or beings...

-clothing is an extension of skin-

-housing is an extension of the body's heat-control mechanism-

-the stirrup, the bicycle, and the car extend the human foot-

-the computer extends our central nervous system-

(Re)Defining "Message"

> HOW, THEN, CAN THE MEDIUM
> BE THE MESSAGE?

By saying "the medium is the message" McLuhan forces us to re-examine what we understand by both "medium" and "message." We have just seen how he stretched the meaning of "medium" beyond our usual understanding of the word. He does this for "message" too. If we define "message" simply as the idea of "content" or "information," McLuhan believes, we miss one of the most important features of media: their power to change the course and functioning of human relations and activities. So, McLuhan redefines the "message" of a medium as any change in scale, pace, or pattern that a medium causes in societies or cultures.

This yields the equation:

MEDIUM = MESSAGE

Another reason for this new definition is that "content" turns out to be an illusion, or at least a mask for how media interact. They work in pairs; one medium "contains" another (and that one can contain another, and so on). The telegraph, for example, contains the printed word, which contains writing, which contains speech. So, the contained medium becomes the message of the containing one!

Now because we don't usually notice this kind of interaction of media, and because the effects of it are so powerful on us, any message, in the ORDINARY sense of "content" or "information" is far less important than the medium itself.

Aha!—you ask—are there no exceptions to media working in pairs? McLuhan points out two:

Media singles

I. Speech

Speech is the content of writing, but what is the content of speech? McLuhan's answer: Speech contains thought, but here the chain of media ends. Thought is non-verbal and pure process.

A second pure process or message-free medium is:

II. The Electric Light

"NO ONE TO TALK TO, ALL BY MYSELF..."

Why does it stand alone?

McLuhan's answer: Artificial light permits activities that could not be conducted in the dark. These activities can be thought of as the "content" of the light, but light itself contains no other medium.

Whether message-containing or message-free, all of the above examples reinforce McLuhan's point that media change the form of human relations and activities. They also reinforce his point about the importance of studying media:

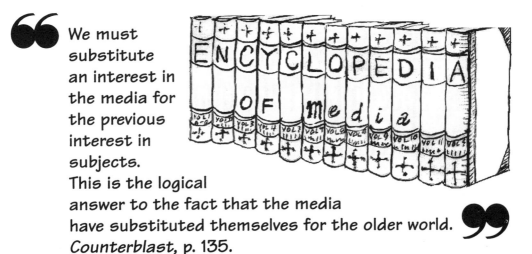

We must substitute an interest in the media for the previous interest in subjects. This is the logical answer to the fact that the media have substituted themselves for the older world. *Counterblast*, p. 135.

Media Gains and Losses

McLuhan saw that media are powerful agents of change that affect how we experience the world, interact with each other, and use our physical senses—the same senses that media themselves extend. He stressed that media must be studied for their **effects**, not their content, because their interaction obscures these effects and deprives us of the power to keep media under our control.

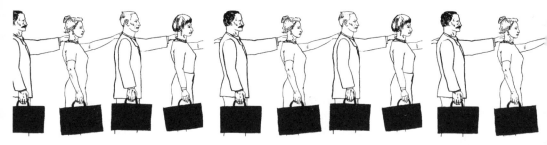

The technology of the age of acoustic space, the technology that later gave writing, print, and telegraph, was speech.

Transformed into writing, speech LOST the quality it had in the age of acoustic space.

It ACQUIRED a powerful visual bias, with effects spilling over into social and cultural organization—and these are still with us today in the electronic age.

But there was also a
SECOND LOSS:

✏—writing separated speech from the other physical senses.

Later, the powerful extension of speech permitted by the development of radio

produced a third LOSS:

—speech was reduced to one sense—the auditory aural.

—RADIO IS NOT SPEECH (BECAUSE WE ONLY LISTEN), BUT IT CREATES THE ILLUSION, LIKE WRITING, OF CONTAINING SPEECH—

So the final score here is one gain and three losses, but we think of the invention of radio as if it were a net gain!

Classifying Media: Hot and Cool

McLuhan's basic classification of media as either "hot" or "cool" hinges on special senses of the words "definition" and "information"—and on our physical senses more than word-senses. McLuhan borrows from the technical language of television to make his point about definition. It's a two-part tale.

Part One:

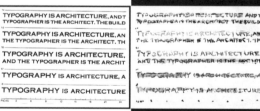

In the TV world, "high-definition" means well-defined, sharp, solid, detailed, etc., in reference to anything visual. So, to McLuhan, letters of the alphabet, numbers, photographs, and maps, for example, are high-definition objects.

Forms and shapes and images that are not so distinct (like sketches and cartoons) are "low-definition." For these, our eyes must scan what is visible and fill in what is missing to "get the full picture." This "fill-in-the-blanks" principle applies to sounds (our sense of hearing) as well. **So**,

A HIGH-DEFINITION MEDIUM

gives a lot of information and gives LITTLE to do *and →*

A LOW-DEFINITION MEDIUM

gives A LITTLE information and makes the user WORK to fill in what is missing

Part Two:

When McLuhan speaks of the "information" that a medium transmits, he is not referring to facts or knowledge; rather, he is referring to how our physical senses respond to, or participate in, media.

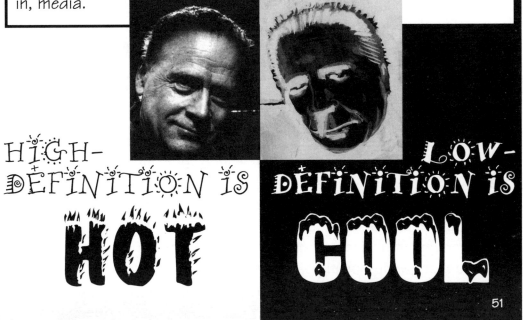

HIGH-DEFINITION IS **HOT**

LOW-DEFINITION IS **COOL**

Here's how McLuhan classifies various media:

HOT

radio

print

photographs

movies

lectures

COOL

telephone

speech

cartoons

television

seminar

gain, McLuhan emphasizes the role of our physical senses and our perceptions and how we relate to media. "Hot" media are low in participation; "cool" media are high in participation. Participation does not refer primarily to intellectual involvement, but, like "definition" and "information," to how a medium engages our physical senses.

Since he was delivering his messages in The Gutenberg Galaxy and Understanding Media via a medium (the printed page) outmoded by the electronic age, McLuhan adopted a style called "mosaic writing" that attempts to mimic the disconnected, low-definition coolness of television. A 1967 Newsweek feature article on McLuhan gave his approach mixed reviews. The article notes that McLuhan's writing is "deliberate, repetitious, confused and dogmatic." Another Newsweek piece gave a somewhat more favorable but still critical review:

> The Gutenberg Galaxy and Understanding Media reflect the synthesis of literature and science. Both books show off McLuhan's appallingly encyclopedic erudition, his exasperating method and the scatter-shot sweep of his theory of culture and communications.

(NOBODY EVER WOULD BELIEVE MCLUHAN WHEN HE INSISTED HE DIDN'T HAVE ANY THEORY.)

Station Break

Before going on, take a minute to review this brief McLuhan "Primer:"

- 📺 No fixed viewpoint

- 📺 No complex, sequential argument

- 📺 No thesis developed over a number of chapters

- 📺 No reliance on linear structure

- 📺 Step into <u>Understanding Media</u> the way you step into a bath...the entry point is of no importance

Narcissus

In *Understanding Media*, McLuhan uses the Greek myth of Narcissus as a dual-purpose metaphor for the failure to understand media as extensions of the human body and the failure to perceive the message (new environments) created by media (technology):

[Narcissus] saw his image reflected in a fountain, and became enamored of it, thinking it to be the nymph of the place. His fruitless attempts to approach this beautiful object so provoked him, that he grew desperate and killed himself.
-*Lemprière's Classical Dictionary*

McLuhan begins by pointing out the common misrepresentation which claims that Narcissus had fallen in love with **himself**. Not so, sayeth our Marshall. It was Narcissus's inability to <u>recognize</u> his image that brought him to grief! The low-tech medium of water and the reflections it allows to form were the culprits! If McLuhan had been around in Narcissus's day, the poor guy would have understood that a little experimenting might have given him control of the medium and allowed him to recognize his own reflection. But, the story goes, Narcissus succumbed to the numbing effect of the sort that McLuhan says all technologies produce, if the user does not scrutinize their operation closely: technologies (new media) create new environments, new environments create pain, and the nervous system shuts down to block the pain. Indeed, McLuhan points out that the name *Narcissus* comes from the Greek word *narcosis*, meaning *numbness*. Narcissus, narcosis. In poor Narcissus's case, the results were fatal.

To McLuhan, the story of Narcissus illustrates humankind's obsessive fascination with new extensions of the body (media), but it also shows how these extensions are inseparable from what McLuhan calls...

Amputations

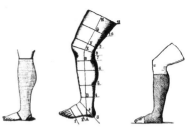

■ake the wheel (as one of McLuhan's examples, that is). As a new technology, the wheel took the pressure of carrying loads off the human foot, which it extends. But it also created new pressure by separating or isolating the function of the foot from other body movements. Whether you are pedalling a bicycle or speeding down the freeway in your car, your foot is performing such a specialized task that you cannot, at that moment, allow it to perform its basic function of walking. So, although the medium has given you the power to move much more quickly, you are, in another sense, immobilized, paralyzed. In this way, our technologies both extend AND amputate.

Amplification becomes amputation. Then the central nervous system reacts to the pressure and disorientation of the amputation by blocking perception.

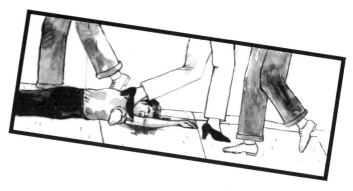

McLuhan used this example to claim that the transition from mechanical to electronic media led to a relentless acceleration—a virtual explosion—of all human activity. But what happens, when media go too far? His answer was simple: Like the overextended highway that turns cities into highways and highways into cities, the technological explosion reverses into an implosion. The expansionist pattern associated with the older technology conflicts with the contracting energies of the new one.

Overheated Media

Remember what McLuhan said about hot and cool media? Well, he also claimed that the vast creative potential unleashed by new media can lead to overheating—sometimes with destructive results. In *Understanding Media*, McLuhan offers examples of overheated media and the reversals they cause. For example, he notes that the industrial Western societies of the nineteenth century placed extreme emphasis on fragmented procedures in the work place.

But, with electrification, both the commercial and social world of industrialized societies began to put new emphasis on unified and unifying forms of organization (corporations, monopolies, clubs, societies). Musings such as these led McLuhan to conclude that electronic technology created a "global village" where knowledge must be synthesized instead of being splintered into specialties. (More on the g.v. later!)

58

Sense ratios

Since McLuhan defines media as extensions of the body, the starting point for his observations about the effects of media on cultures and societies is always the human individual. As a result, two questions McLuhan probed in great depth were:

> TO WHAT EXTENT DO HUMANS DEPEND ON ONE SENSE RELATIVE TO ANOTHER?

> AND

> WHAT HAPPENS WHEN THAT RATIO IS MODIFIED?

cLuhan argued that the introduction of new media alters what he called our sense ratio, or the relationship among the five physical senses. He further argued that the senses may be ranked in order of how complex the perceptions are that we get through them.

Sight comes first, he claimed, because the eye is a specialized organ that permits perceptions of enormous complexity. Then come hearing, touch, smell and taste.

Reading down the list, we move to less specialized senses. By contrast with the enormous power of the eye and the distances from which it can receive a stimulus, the tongue is capable of distinguishing only sweet, sour, bitter, and salt, and only in direct contact with the substance providing the stimulus.

Because any modifications to our sense ratio inevitably involve a psychological dimension, McLuhan cautioned against any rigid separation of the physical from the psychological—perhaps in all analysis, but especially for an understanding of media and their effects.

TAKE THE INVENTION OF THE ALPHABET, FOR EXAMPLE.

(MCLUHAN DID!)

McLuhan alleged that the resulting intensification of the visual sense—and reliance on it—in the communication process swamped hearing so force-fully that the effect spilled over from language and com-munication to reshape liter-ate society's conception of space. Here are further examples, where McLuhan stresses sense ratios and the effects of altering them:

In dentistry, a device called audiac was developed. It con-sists of headphones bombarding the patient with enough noise to block pain from the dentist's drill.

In Hollywood, the addition of sound to silent pictures impoverished and gradually eliminated the role of mime, with its tactility and kines-thesis.

SPARE CHANGE?

The Microphone at Mass

McLuhan believes that when the microphone was introduced into Catholic churches it brought about the demystification of things spiritual for many believers. The introduction of a new technology started a chain reaction: First the Latin mass, as a "cool" medium, was rendered obsolete, because it is unsuited to amplification. (A hot medium can be overheated or overextended, and this intensification can make the medium more effective, but a cool one, when overheated, becomes less effective.) Next came the obsolescence of traditional church architecture, the decline in the use of incense (knocking out the sense of smell) and the disappearance of the rosary (eliminating the tactile sense).

What McLuhan calls the "audio backdrop" of Latin used to provide an invitation to intense participation through meditation as the priest said mass. This was replaced by the high-definition medium of the mass in the vernacular, required by and then intensified still further by the use of microphones and loudspeakers, but no longer requiring intense sensory or spiritual involvement. As for the cathedral architecture, with its shape and dimensions dictated for centuries by the acoustical requirements of a non-electronically amplified voice, it became as obsolete as Latin.

Rubbing media together

Everyone knows that friction, caused by rubbing two items together, creates heat. Like friction, McLuhan claimed, combining media unleashes powerful forces, but neither the creation of such energy nor the experience of it brings about an awareness of what is happening. That's because media mask each other when they interact.

But

McLuhan is optimistic that media consciousness can be raised by following appropriate strategies. To illustrate, he turned to Edgar Allen Poe's "A Descent into the Maelstrom." In this story, a sailor rescues himself from the whirlpool engulfing him by calmly observing its effects on the various objects caught in the downward spiral. The sailor's attitude of rational detachment allows him to find a means of escape and even intellectual amusement in the midst of the environment that threatens his life.

Media effects are just as inescapable as the whirlpool of the story, McLuhan contends, BUT detached analysis of their operation can bring freedom from their numbing effects.

IN OTHER WORDS, MCLUHAN'S STRATEGY IS THIS: BEFORE WE CAN SAVE OURSELVES FROM DROWNING IN THE MEDIA OF OUR OWN CREATION, WE MUST FIRST OBSERVE AND THEN UNDERSTAND THEM.

Such analysis is never easier, says McLuhan, than when two media meet, yielding the equation:

MEDIUM + MEDIUM = MESSAGE

To drive home this point, McLuhan turns again to the example of electricity, but he also uses the metaphor of violent energy —the fission of the atomic bomb and the fusion of the hydrogen bomb—to speculate on the final outcome of these changes. It's changes in cultures and societies that occupy McLuhan most fully (pre-literate, non-Western cultures are fragmented by the introduction of writing; visual, specialist, Western culture is retribalized by electricity), but he offers other examples:

⚡ When the telegraph restructured the press medium, human interest stories, previously the preserve of the theater, were introduced into newspapers, causing the decline of theater.

⚡ For just a moment before an airplane breaks the sound barrier, sound waves become visible on its wings. Then they disappear as the plane moves into the new environment beyond the speed of sound. It is a metaphor for the moment when the structure of a medium is revealed as it meets with another.

When media combine, McLuhan observes, they establish new ratios among themselves, just as they establish new ratios among the senses. For example,

👁 When radio came along, it changed the way news stories were presented and the way film images were presented in the talkies 👁

👁 then television came along and brought big changes in radio 👁

In a nutshell:

—When media combine, both their form and use change—

—so do the scale, speed, and intensity of the human endeavors affected, as well as the ratios of senses involved—

—so do the environments where the media and their users are found—

IT'S A TRIPLE PLAY!!
NEW MEDIA TO NEW SENSORY BALANCE
TO NEW ENVIRONMENT!!

Let's test McLuhan's ideas by taking an example of technology that was not available in his time. For instance:

The optical scanner

The optical scanner reads and reproduces texts or images with great speed and accuracy (especially in the case of images that otherwise would have to be created by free-hand reproduction). As a writing medium, it renders obsolete all the non-hybridized and non-electronic technologies that preceded it, from the quill to the typewriter, AND the hand that uses them. As a powerful visual technology, and because it is hybridized, the scanner reduces its users to proof-readers and document managers. So, the scanner is a hybrid extension of the eye and the hand.

The Alphabet

e write English in what is called a "phonetic" alphabet. The letters of our alphabet stand for sounds. A phonetic alphabet is a medium, as McLuhan defines medium (remember?—a medium is any extension of our bodies or minds).

The phonetic alphabet is an extension of BOTH our bodies and our minds, because:

A

👄 it turns the sounds of language that we make with our lungs and tongues and teeth and lips into visual markings— *and*

E

👄 the sounds extend or "outer" (="utter"—a pun McLuhan loved) the thoughts in our minds.

I

We've also got media working in pairs here again!!

O

So, the phonetic alphabet is a medium, because it's an extension, BUT it's also a medium in the basic sense of "something that goes between" — AND BRINGS TOGETHER. What does the alphabet go between and bring together? Answer: MEANING and SOUND.

U

If we compare, say, Chinese writing with the phonetic alphabet, there is no "go-between" for Chinese. The writing gives meanings, but it doesn't show how to pronounce what is written.

If you are having trouble understanding this, think about symbols like

There is nothing in the shapes of these symbols to show how they are pronounced, but there is in

plus and minus.

Imagine if EVERY written word in English was a symbol like

"+" instead of "plus"
"&" instead of "and"
"-" instead of "minus"

and then you've got an idea of how Chinese writing works.(I think I hear a reader going !@#%* Very non-phonetic. You ARE getting it!)

	EGYPTIAN	PHŒNICIAM		GREEK				LATIN			HEBREW
1	🦅	∠	Δ	A	A	ʌ	α	A	A	ɑ a a	א
2		ʒ	৭	৪	B	B	β	ß	B	B b	ב
3	⊿	Z	٦	٦	Γ	Γ	✓γ	‹	C	C Gc g g	ג
4		→	Δ	Δ	Δ	ᛌ	δ	D	D	ᛞ ᛞ d	ד
5	⊓	⊞	ৰ	₹	E	E	ε	ᛒ	E	e e	ה
6	↤	⁄	Ꮞ	Ꮞ	YF		F	F	F	ᚠ f	ו
7	🦎	₴	ⅉ	‡	I	Z	ᵹ ᵹ	‡	Z	z	ז
8	⊙	⌒	日	日	H	H	h η	日	H	h h	ח
9	⚍	⊷	⊕	⊕	⊙	Θ	θ ᎐	⊗			ט
10	⑾	৴	Ꮞ	৲	∤	١	١	١	I	i j	⅃
11	⌒	٩	५	ⅎ	K	K	ĸ κ	K	K	k	כ
12	⌘	₵	L	v	∧	λ	λ	L	L	l	⅃
		ๅ	M	M	M	M	μ μ	M	M	m m	מ
		⅄	Ꮢ	Ꮢ	N	N	ν ν	Ꮢ	N	n n	נ
		‡	Ξ	℥	Ξ		⊞	+	x x		ס
	∘	O	O	O	O	o	O		O	o	ע
	⅂	Γ	π	π ϖ	P	P	P		פ
		⋈	M		ᵌ	Ᵽ				צ
		Q			Q	Q q q			ק
		P	P	ᵱ ᵱ	Ᵽ	R	ᵱ r		ר
		W	⊆	C	⊏ σ	⸦	S	⸏ ʃ s		ש
22	٥	Ⴆ	✝	T	T	Τ τ	Τ	Τ ᴄ t		ת
1	II	III	IV	V	VI	VII	VIII IX	x	XI		

69

McLuhan understood that the EFFECTS of a phonetic alphabet are very different from those of non-phonetic writing and very powerful. He sees the invention of the phonetic alphabet as having set off a chain reaction that gave Western civilization everything from logic and linear space to nationalism and assembly lines.

McLuhan finds a lesson on the power of media once again in Greek mythology. It was king Cadmus who planted dragon's teeth from which an army sprang up. It was also Cadmus who introduced the phonetic alphabet (from Phoenicia) to Greece.

McLuhan interprets the dragon's teeth as an older form of non-phonetic writing from which the much more powerful alphabet grew

Media Metaphors

Remember the immortal words of poet Robert Browning:

"AH, BUT A MAN'S REACH SHOULD EXCEED HIS GRASP, OR WHAT'S A HEAVEN FOR?"

Robert Browning

True to form, McLuhan turns these words on their head in probing media messages with a tongue-in-cheek phrase of his own:

"A MAN'S REACH MUST EXCEED HIS GRASP OR WHAT'S A METAPHOR?" (UNDERSTANDING MEDIA, P. 57)

71

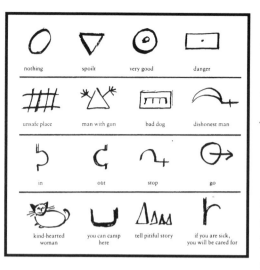

nothing	spoilt	very good	danger
unsafe place	man with gun	bad dog	dishonest man
in	out	stop	go
kind-hearted woman	you can camp here	tell pitiful story	if you are sick, you will be cared for

If we take the "reach" and the "grasp" in McLuhan's quip as mental rather than physical, the question contains its answer, just as McLuhan claims that media contain each other.

McLuhan saw it this way: In language, a metaphor is an extension of consciousness, a medium in the broad sense that is fundamental for McLuhan. When we look beyond language,

ALL media are active metaphors, or technologies for transforming human experience.

According to our Marshall, until electronic media became the dominant technology, the transformations of human experience were those of the human body mechanically extended. Now they are of human consciousness electronically extended. Activities previously performed only by electro-chemical energy in the human brain can now be performed by electromagnetic energy in the computer.

The result: we—individuals, societies, nations, schools, businesses, citizens of the global village—are transformed into information systems. So powerful is the technology of the computer, McLuhan cautioned more than twenty years ago, that it would be possible to transform and store <u>anything</u>, including all our knowledge of ourselves.

STARTLED BY THE PROSPECT OF YOUR HEALTHY BODY TURNING INTO AN INFORMATION SYSTEM OR DISAPPEARING FOREVER INTO A COMPUTER?

A bit of word-play here may help to ease your mind. "Information" is whatever is "in formation," that is, defined by its relation to something else. Any transformation is stored as information. So the medium is not only the message, it's the metaphor, too!

The Money is the Metaphor

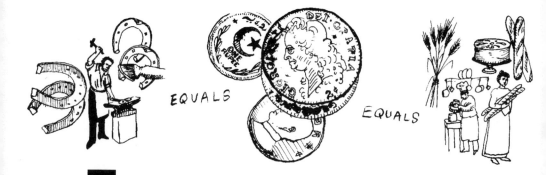

EQUALS   EQUALS

Money is a medium as much as the alphabet, because it provides a means of exchange. The alphabet allows exchange of words and ideas; money allows exchange of commodities and services. Money can also be a commodity in itself when objects that are valued serve as a medium of exchange.

Whales' teeth, tulip bulbs, and tobacco have all been used as money. A major activity in the financial world is trading where the commodity on the market is the medium of money itself. Bank advertising refers to "financial products" as if money-related services were tangible commodities.

McLuhan stresses several paral-
lels between money and language:

◎ Language develops in the child as the physical grasping reflex is replaced by a mental grasp
of the environment, provided by words. In the
same way, the concept of money as currency
rather than commodity evolved when the grasp
on commodities was relaxed to allow trading ◎

◎ Money shares with writing the power to
focus and redirect human energy and to
isolate the functions of the human body in
the same way that it transforms work ◎

◎ Writing eroded the magic of the spoken work, just as printed money under-
mined the aura of gold and silver coins ◎

◎ Money and language are both reposito-
ries of work, skill, and experience that
derive from community ◎

◎ Writing and money are both hot media,
intensifying speech and isolating work from
other social functions respectively ◎

In view of these similari-
ties between money and
language, it is not sur-
prising that we say
"MONEY TALKS!"

The Key to the Car

Because of mankind's obsession with motion, civilization has been marked by one technology after another extending the human foot. The invention of the wheel eventually led, among others, to the bicycle, the motorcycle, the train, the airplane, and the car. While the motorcycle may be more personal and the airplane more powerful, none of these media has produced such a set of psychological, cultural, and socio-economic effects (through the creation of a huge service environment) as the car.

Agent of stress, status symbol, transformer of country landscape and cityscapes alike. These features of the car were well understood before McLuhan turned his attention to it.

His analysis focuses elsewhere:

◎ Cars are the population of the city cores they have transformed, and the result has been a loss of human scale ◎

◎ The car is neither less nor more of a sex object than other technologies. It is mankind that functions as the sex organ of all technologies by creating and cross-fertilizing them ◎

◎ The demise of the car began with television, because it undermines the uniformity and standardization of assembly-line production with which the car is identified ◎

◎ Acceptance of the limousine as a status symbol, associated with wealth and power, is not an indication of the mechanical age that spawned the car but of the electronic age bringing the older one to a close and redefining status and role ◎

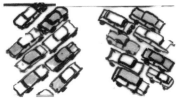

For McLuhan, such observations are the key to understanding the car as a medium in relation to other media and their effects on each other and on society.

Art for our sake

TOULOUSE - LAUTREC

The numbing effect of new media is caused by a shift in sense ratios, McLuhan says. The shift sets in automatically with the arrival of new technologies and acts as a sort of local anaesthetic to make technological change less painful. McLuhan speaks of "huge collective surgery" (*Understanding Media*, p. 64) carried out on society with the implantation of the new media.

McLuhan goes even further with his medical metaphor: infection can set in during the operation and threaten the whole body, so some measure to provide immunity is called for.

THE HOPE OF IMMUNIZING SOCIETY COMES FROM THE ARTIST, WHO DETECTS THE CHANGES IN THE WIND RESULTING FROM NEW TECHNOLOGIES LONG BEFORE THEY EXERT THEIR FULL IMPACT.

Result:

ART FUNCTIONS AS AN ANTI-ENVIRONMENTAL CONTROL

Alien Staff

video screen

metal
head
w/video
on top

sound
vents

Side
View

wood
or
ribbed
rubber

Glass
capsule
for
display
of
personal
artifacts
and
legal
papers

*

In other words, art protects society from the new environment that technological innovations create, from the inevitable epidemic sweep that follows the introduction of new technology.

McLuhan points out that the French symbolist poets of the late nineteenth century were entirely in harmony with the new breakthroughs in science:

quantum mechanics, non-Euclidean geometry, relativity theory

ALBERT EINSTEIN AND ROBERT OPPENHEIMER

The poets and the scientists were in agreement in seeing RESONANCE as the fundamental quality of the universe.

As for James Joyce (maybe McLuhan's all-time favorite), he understood that the EFFECT of electricity would be the reunification of the physical SENSES and the RETRIBALIZATION of Western culture.

Electronic Pentecost

McLuhan sees no salvation coming from the televangelists, but he speculates on the potential that electronic technology holds for recreating the Pentecostal experience in the global village. The tongues of fire that empowered believers on the day of Pentecost is not just part of the imagery that McLuhan carried with him as a devout Roman Catholic. Fire is the ancient symbol of becoming, of transformation, of transcendence, and so of the power of the Holy Spirit and the power of a medium, combined at Pentecost in language.

McLuhan refers to language as:

> *"THE FIRST TECHNOLOGY BY WHICH MAN WAS ABLE TO LET GO OF HIS ENVIRONMENT IN ORDER TO GRASP IT IN A NEW WAY."*
> *(UNDERSTANDING MEDIA, P. 57)*

Language is:

➤ **the technology that has both translated (thought into speech) and been translated by other technologies throughout the course of civilisation (hieroglyphics, phonetic alphabet, printing press, telegraph, phonograph, radio and telephone)**◄

➤ **central to McLuhan's teachings on media, their transformations, and interactions**◄

➤ **central to the French symbolist poets who saw language as decayed past the point of allowing a new Pentecost.**◄

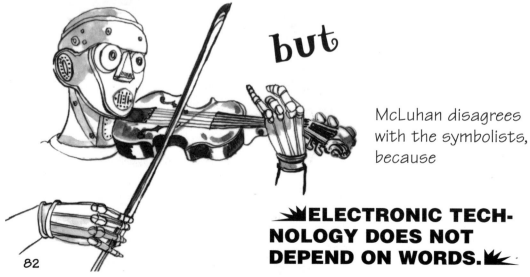

but

McLuhan disagrees with the symbolists, because

➤ **ELECTRONIC TECHNOLOGY DOES NOT DEPEND ON WORDS.**◄

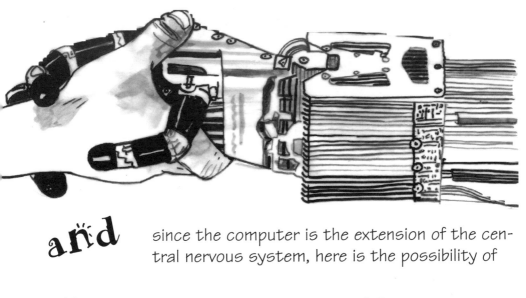

and since the computer is the extension of the central nervous system, here is the possibility of

extending consciousness without verbalization,

getting past the fragmentation and numbing effect of language,

A WAY TO UNIVERSAL UNDERSTANDING AND UNITY.

... sounds familiar ...

Dali Lama

Comparing Media

Despite its title, *Understanding Media* is not an easy work to understand. In the 1994 reissue of the book, however, Lewis Lapham presents a neat little side-by-side comparison that reduces McLuhan's assessments of the characteristics of print and electronic media to their lowest common denominators (pp. xii-xiii):

Print Media

visual
mechanical
sequence
composition
eye
active
expansion
complete
soliloquy
classification
center
continuous
syntax
self-expression
Typographic Man

Electronic Media

tactile
organic
simultaneity
improvisation
ear
reactive
contraction
incomplete
chorus
pattern recognition
margin
discontinuous
mosaic
group therapy
Graphic Man

THERE NOW, DOESN'T THAT HELP??!!

Lights, Action,...: McLuhan on Television

After *Understanding Media*, McLuhan collaborated with Quentin Fiore on *The Medium is the Massage: An Inventory of Effects* (1967). One critic, who calls this work "the million-selling, McLuhan Made Easy paperback," notes also that it "eroded [McLuhan's] reputation among the intelligentsia even as it secured it among the masses" (Dery, 1995, p. 24).

Marshall McLuhan
Author of UNDERSTANDING MEDIA
Quentin Fiore
The Medium is the Massage
An Inventory of Effects

CULTURAL REPUTATION CHART

LES INTELLECTUALS

McLuhan

THE WORKING STIFFS

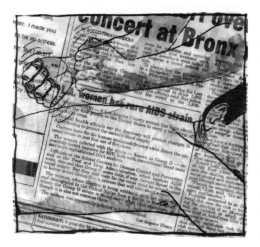

The pun in the title underscores both McLuhan's unwillingness to take himself too seriously and his characteristically witty ideas about the most far-reaching of media effects, that of creating complete—and completely new—environments for society. To quote McLuhan, like the masseuse, "all media work us over completely." The metaphor is also linked to McLuhan's observations that art, not media, provides a means for societies and individuals to recover from the numbing, massage-like effect created when the body of society is touched at every point by technological innovation.

When
information
is
brushed
against
information...

When
information
is
brushed
against
information...

Mosaic Man and "All-at-Onceness"

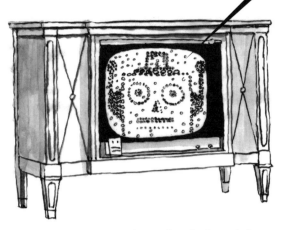

In *Massage*, McLuhan likens the image on a television screen to a flat, two-dimensional mosaic. Unlike the hot medium of print, he contends, the TV mosaic does not have a visual structure that allows the eye to race in a straight line over sharply defined forms. It does not have uniform, continuous, or repetitive features, nor does it extend sight to the exclusion of the other senses. Rather, he claimed that TV has a tactile quality—discontinuous and nonlinear—like the features of a mosaic. Television images, though received by the eye, were viewed by McLuhan as primarily extensions of the sense of touch. The image on the screen has the type of texture associated with touch. Additionally, while it provides a minimum of information, television creates an interplay of all the senses at once, whereas print media separate and fragment the physical senses.

It was this all-at-onceness, he claimed, that forced....the GREAT DIVIDE... A shift from:

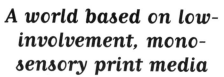

A world based on low-involvement, mono-sensory print media

[LOOK OUT BELOW!!]

A world based on high-involvement, multisensory electronic media

McLuhan argued that with the introduction of television in the 1950s, the abstract-visual sense that had dominated Western culture for centuries through the alphabet and printing press was abruptly dislocated. The impact of such a reorganization was particularly strong in North America and England, whose cultures had been intensely literate for so long. The changes in social trends and values influenced by television were immediate and profound. As McLuhan points out:

ON BOTH SIDES OF THE ATLANTIC, LANGUAGE TEACHING CHANGED; KNOWLEDGE OBTAINED BY READING ALONE WAS NO LONGER FAVORED. TV CREATED A TASTE FOR ALL EXPERIENCE IN DEPTH AND ALL AT ONCE.

EUROPE BEGAN AMERICANIZING AS QUICKLY AS NORTH AMERICA BEGAN EUROPEANIZING.

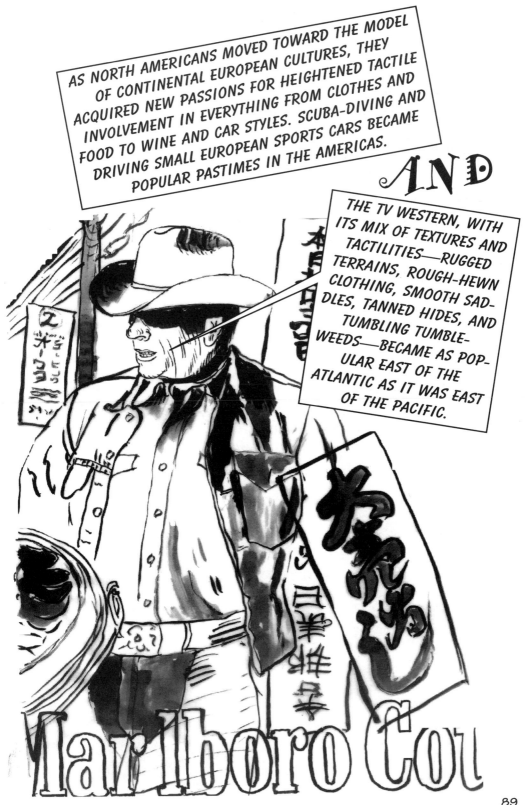

AS NORTH AMERICANS MOVED TOWARD THE MODEL OF CONTINENTAL EUROPEAN CULTURES, THEY ACQUIRED NEW PASSIONS FOR HEIGHTENED TACTILE INVOLVEMENT IN EVERYTHING FROM CLOTHES AND FOOD TO WINE AND CAR STYLES. SCUBA-DIVING AND DRIVING SMALL EUROPEAN SPORTS CARS BECAME POPULAR PASTIMES IN THE AMERICAS.

AND

THE TV WESTERN, WITH ITS MIX OF TEXTURES AND TACTILITIES—RUGGED TERRAINS, ROUGH-HEWN CLOTHING, SMOOTH SADDLES, TANNED HIDES, AND TUMBLING TUMBLE-WEEDS—BECAME AS POPULAR EAST OF THE ATLANTIC AS IT WAS EAST OF THE PACIFIC.

Marlboro Cou

Further, McLuhan claimed that television's (and other high speed electronic media's) all-at-onceness—its ability to transmit images and information from a variety of sources, places, and times—prompted the world to contract into a "global village in which everyone is involved with everyone else—the haves with the have-nots,...Negroes with whites,...adults with teen-agers." On television, McLuhan noted, everything everywhere happens simultaneously, with no clear order or sequence. He credited the medium with a wide range of changes in the American social and political scene:

> **Television brings not only the voting booth into the living room but also the civil-rights march along Alabama's U.S. 80 and the bull-dozing of a village in Vietnam-and involves the audience intimately...**

> **Without television, there would be no civil-rights legislation.**

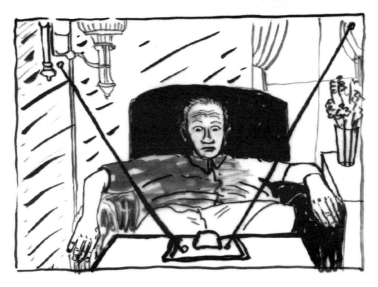

McLuhan also noted a strange paradox: TV viewers' high involvement with the images projected on the screen minimized rather than heightened the need of viewers to respond to what they see on TV. For example:

" The Kennedy event [the 1963 funeral of slain President John F. Kennedy] provides an opportunity for noting a paradoxical feature of the 'cool' TV medium. It involves us in moving depth, but it does not excite, agitate or arouse. "

...a hot war like Vietnam over a cool medium like TV is doomed. The young oppose the war not out of pacifism but out of the pain of involvement [with television images of the war].

 Since TV, the whole American political temperature has cooled down, down, down, until the political process is almost approaching rigor mortis.

Connecting the Dots

McLuhan observed that the television screen is a mesh of dots through which light shines with varying intensity to allow an image to form—but not before the spaces in the mesh are "closed." He referred to this process of closure as "a convulsive sensuous participation that is profoundly kinetic and tactile" (*Understanding Media*, p. 314) [Wow! Remember, touch was one of McLuhan's all-time "pick" senses!] But, to McLuhan, closure did not refer merely to closing up the spaces in the mesh of dots on the television screen, but to the closing down of one physical sense when another is extended by a new medium.

Closure, of the television sort, also marked for McLuhan a shift toward a new balance among our senses: while television reawakens our tactile sense, it diminishes the visual sense relied upon in a purely print culture and replaces it with an all-encompassing sensory experience. There is, of course, no contact between the skin of the viewer and the television, but, according to McLuhan, the eye is so much more intensely engaged by the television screen than by print that the effect is the same as that of touching!

McLuhan saw a down-side to this sensory closure thing, however, claiming that it causes conformity to the pattern of experience presented by a medium. He issued a sterner warning in *Understanding Media*, likening TV to a disease:

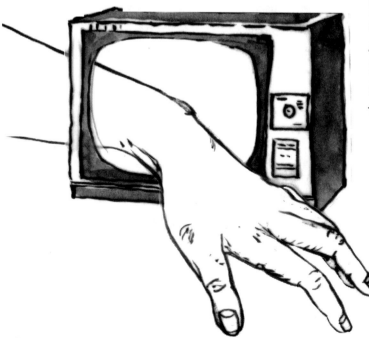

his warning also shows us that to take McLuhan as a promoter of television is to miss an important part of his teaching. Indeed, he cautioned that not even his insights into the operation and power of media could offset "the ordinary 'closure' of the senses" (*Understanding Media*). And remember, he didn't want his own grandkids growing up glued to the tube!

Television "Types"

MOTHER TERESA

AL SHARPTON

McLuhan had lots to say about who (the kinds of people) or what (the kind of image) were most suitable for television. TV viewers, he claimed, because of the sensory involvement the medium demands and the habits of perception it imposes, come to expect not a "fixed" image but one they are required to "fix." Thus, persons who represent a "type"—that is, those whose physical appearances make a statement about their role and status in life—overheat the cool medium of TV, depriving its viewers of the task of closure. Successful TV personalities, McLuhan claimed, were those whose appearance fed the medium's need for texture with (for example):

HIGHLY STYLIZED HAIR
(MOUSTACHES, BEARDS)
SMALL NOSES

LARGE TEETH
CRAGGY BROWS
HIGH CHEEKBONES

GENE SHALIT

J.F.K

TALKING HEADS

However, McLuhan allowed that persons who are neither shaggy, craggy, nor sculptured could nevertheless project an acceptable television presence—if they fed the cool medium's other fundamental need: for free-flowing chat and dialogue. This explained, to McLuhan, at least, why, in the earliest days of television, someone like talk show host

✳✳Jack Paar✳✳

AND THE TALK SHOW FORMAT ITSELF WAS, AND REMAINS, SO POPULAR.

ORIGINAL TALKING HEAD

TV as Teaching Tool

McLuhan drew no sharp distinctions between television's role as an entertainment medium and as an educational tool. He did note, however, that traditional pedagogical techniques, developed during the Print Age and incorporating all the visual biases of print, became less effective with the advent of television. He called for greater understanding of the dynamics of this powerful medium, its action on our senses, and its interaction with other media. Simply showing teachers teaching on TV, he claimed, was a useless overheating of the cool medium of television. Yet, there were some things he believed television could do that the classroom could not: "TV can illustrate the interplay of process and the growth of forms of all kinds as nothing else can" (*Understanding Media*, p. 332). He advised teachers "not only to understand the television medium but to exploit it for its pedagogical richness" (*Understanding Media*, p. 335).

The Medium Is The Mess-age

Lewis Lapham, in the Introduction to the thirtieth anniversary edition of *Understanding Media,* summarizes McLuhan's insights about advertising:

> McLuhan notices, correctly, that it is the bad news—reports of sexual scandal, natural disaster, and violent death—that sells the good news—that is, the advertisements. The bad news is the spiel that brings the suckers into the tent....The homily is as plain as a medieval morality play or the bloodstains on ["Miami Vice" star] Don Johnson's Armani suit—obey the law, pay your taxes, speak politely to the police officer, and you go to the Virgin Islands on the American Express card. Disobey the law, neglect your insurance payments, speak rudely to the police, and you go to Kings County Hospital in a body bag."

REMEMBER...
DON'T LEAVE HOME WITHOUT IT.

McLuhan's *Culture Is Our Business* did for the advertising of the 1960s what *The Mechanical Bride* did for the advertising of the 1940s. McLuhan argued that the advent and impact of television made the update necessary. The book, like most of McLuhan's work, received mixed reviews, but some advertising executives, like Howard Gossage, one of McLuhan's most ardent converts and supporters, were enthusiastic. (Gossage heralded McLuhan as "an Archimedes who has given the ad industry levers to move the world.")

The basic premise of the 1970 book lies in its title, which is best understood if read both forward and backward—that is, the new information environment created by the electronic age transforms business into culture and culture into business.

CULTURE IS OUR BUSINESS =
BUSINESS IS OUR CULTURE

In this book, McLuhan waxes poetical, if only briefly, on modern-day television ads, calling them "the cave art of the twentieth century" (1) because they are not intended to be examined in detail but to create an effect, and (2) because they express not private thoughts but rather corporate aims. Again, he uses the mosaic, television-like approach found in virtually all of his works, pushing it to its most whimsical and thought-provoking extremes. *Culture Is Our Business* is comprised of hundreds of ads. But only rarely does McLuhan offer any comment on them. Instead, he simply positions most of the ads side-by-side with questions to the reader, factual statements that probe the claims and significance of the ads, or quotations and observations from writers as diverse as James Joyce (always a McLuhan favorite), T. S. Eliot, William Congreve, Alfred North Whitehead, Ashley Montagu, and Karl Polanyi.

MERCEDES-BENZ

I love cool colours with a sizzle

The Global Village

cLuhan's more optimistic musings about the psychic effects of television, computers, and sophisticated telecommunications media, coupled with his ideas about the retribalizing effects of electronic media, led him to posit the existence of a "global village." In an interview published in *Playboy* magazine in 1969, he noted that he saw the reconfigured world environment emerging as a result of humankind's increasingly intense interaction with electronic media as one in which "the human tribe can become truly one family and man's consciousness can be freed from the shackles of mechanical culture and enabled to roam the cosmos."

Contemporary critics dispel McLuhan's vision of the global village as seriously off the mark. Rather than open up the world and improve the interactions of those within it, they point out that the rise of "one-world pop-tech civilization" has done exactly the opposite. As a *Village Voice* article noted, the cybernatization of media

66 **has offered people the opportunity to pack themselves into ever smaller worlds, where enthusiasms mutate into obsessions, and a reality check is a parallel dimension away. 99**

However, even McLuhan realized that his utopian vision, with its "depth-structured" global citizens, came at a price:

> "There is more diversity, less conformity under a single roof in any family than there is with the thousands of families in the same city. The more you create village conditions, the more discontinuity and division and diversity. The global village absolutely insures maximal disagreement on all points. It never occurred to me that uniformity and tranquillity were the properties of the global village....The tribal-global village is far more divisive—full of fighting—than any nationalism ever was. Village is fission, not fusion, in depth....The village is not the place to find ideal peace and harmony. Exact opposite." (from "A Dialogue: Q & A" in Gerald E. Stearn, ed., *McLuhan Hot and Cool*)

DISORDERED STATES, CIVIL WARS + ETHNIC CONFLICTS *

* U.S. REPORTS ON HUMAN RIGHTS FOR 1993 (Except L.A)

Noting that the nationalism created b
of print media provided an extraordina
the conditions of feudalism and tribal
ceded it, McLuhan maintained that he
violent social upheavals and renewed ir
conflicts of the global village "with tot
dislike and dissatisfaction."

McLuhan:

**"*I don't approve o
global village. I s
live in it.*"**

Hmmmm,
nice place

From Cliche to Archetype

After doing a lot of mosaic writing, McLuhan turned around and published what seems to be set up like a mini-encyclopedia—From *Cliché to Archetype* (1970). But it turns out to be a put-on! It's just as much a mosaic as his other books, and when you stop to think about it, he packs so much into those books that they are like encyclopedias too. It's all a trick to get us thinking about the ideas packed into the title—clichés and archetypes—what they are and how they interact.

...COME HERE OFTEN?

Most readers will recognize **cliché** as meaning a worn-out expression, but what is an archetype? McLuhan explores the various meanings of **archetype**, but it is useful for us to start with a general, basic definition:

ARCHETYPE, LIKE TYPE, REFERS TO A PATTERN OR MODEL.

In literature an archetype is a symbol or image (person, place, or thing) that we recognize because we meet the type repeatedly:

CALL ME MOBY...

Flipper

HEROES FROM BEOWULF TO BATMAN

EARTHLY PARADISES FROM EDEN TO SHANGRI-LA

ut we meet clichés repeatedly too. It's because they are repeated so often that they are clichés. So we see already why McLuhan emphasizes the connection between cliché and archetype.

Meet CAPTAIN AMERICA

An archetype is a category you can add to (the more you have read, the more names you can add to those of Beowulf and Batman); a cliché is not a category, and you cannot add to it. But you can change it, and we will see what McLuhan has to say about how this is done in the hands of artists.

We saw how McLuhan stretched the sense of "medium"; he does the same with "cliché", defining it at different times as:

➤an extension,
➤a probe,
➤a means of retrieving the past.

These are echoes of important notions from McLuhan's other writings. They show us how central the cliché is in his analysis.

McLuhan goes so far as to say that our perceptions are clichés (because our physical senses are a closed system), that all communications media are clichés (because they extend our physical senses), and that art is cliché (because it retrieves older clichés).

The simplest definition of cliché for McLuhan is that of a probe. This may sound like a paradox (especially if we go back to the definition of cliché as a worn-out expression), and McLuhan admits that this is so. BUT, what happens is that artists sharpen clichés into probes, into new forms that jolt us into awareness. The familiar, even the worn-out, becomes new.

As usual, one of McLuhan's favorites to illustrate this point is James Joyce, who wakes up language (creates new clichés) by putting it to sleep (destroying old clichés). We hear the echo of

"give an inch and take a mile"

when Joyce writes

"GIVEN NOW ANN LINCH YOU TAKE ENN ALL";

we catch the clichés

"skin of his teeth" and **"earned his bread"**

transformed into probes that call up the myth of King Cadmus when Joyce writes "He dug in and dug out by the skill of his tilth for himself and all belonging to him and he sweated his crew beneath his auspice and he urned his dread".

Archetypes both interact and contrast with clichés. McLuhan defines the archetype as a retrieved awareness or new consciousness. This happens when the artist probes an archetype with an old cliché, as in the examples from James Joyce above. Sooner or later, the probe itself turns into a cliché. McLuhan views all form, whether in language, visual arts, music, etc., as a reversing of archetype into cliché. But cliché also reverses into archetype.

Let's give McLuhan himself the last word on the subject:

"THE ARCHETYPE IS A RETRIEVED AWARENESS OR CONSCIOUSNESS. IT IS CONSEQUENTLY A RETRIEVED CLICHÉ—AND OLD CLICHÉ RETRIEVED BY A NEW CLICHÉ. SINCE A CLICHÉ IS A UNIT EXTENSION OF MAN, AN ARCHETYPE IS A QUOTED EXTENSION, MEDIUM, TECHNOLOGY, OR ENVIRONMENT." (FROM CLICHÉ TO ARCHETYPE, P. 21)

The Mechanical Bride

COMIC STRIPS

The comics engage McLuhan's attention as a reflection of popular culture (and as an example of a "cool" medium). Some comic strips he condemns, others he praises. The point, in either case, is to create a full awareness of the biases the strips adopt, the models they use, and the values they perpetuate.

In Little Orphan Annie, McLuhan sees the American success story grounded in the psychological need to achieve that success by both pleasing parents **and** outdoing them. Voluntary orphanhood. Its frightening aspects of isolation and helplessness are mitigated by Annie's character—her innocence and her goodness—and, of course, by her success in doing battle, as valiantly as Joan of Arc, against incompetence, interference, stupidity, and evil.

The adventures of Superman, McLuhan observes, go beyond tales of the science-fiction type to dramatize the psychological defeat of technological man. Always the victor when sheer force can bring the victory, Superman is nothing but the alter *ego* of the incompetent and vilified Clark Kent, a wish fulfillment in a man whose persona suggests to McLuhan a society reacting to the pressures of the technological age, rejecting civilizing processes such as due process of law, and embracing violence.

It is significant that Tarzan, like Superman, has an alter ego in the person of Lord Greystoke. By contrast with the downtrodden Clark Kent, Greystoke is what McLuhan calls "the unreconstructed survivor of the wreck of feudalism." (*The Mechanical Bride*, p. 104) He is outside the duality of noble savage/civilized man, an aristocrat who forsook the salon for the jungle, a hybrid in whom the ideals of the Y.M.C.A., Kipling, and Baden-Powell come together.

CONCEALMENT NO LONGER POSSIBLE, TARZAN SPRANG FORWARD. THE GREAT KNIFE WHISTLED ABOVE HIS HEAD AS THE SAVAGE CRY OF THE GREAT APES RE-ECHOED THROUGH THE CAVERN.

McLuhan's least favorite strip was Blondie, because it was pure formula—repetitive and predictable. Dagwood is trapped in suburban life, frustrated, and victimized. He gets little sympathy from his children and none from McLuhan. Where readers might find Dagwood's midnight trips to the refrigerator comical, McLuhan finds them contemptible: "promiscuous gormandizing as a basic dramatic symbol of the abused and the insecure." (*The Mechanical Bride*, p. 68) Unlike Jiggs, in Bringing Up Father, who belongs to the first generation of his family to have realized the American dream, Dagwood is second generation and lacking the competitiveness that motivated his father to realize that dream. Nearly fifty years ago, McLuhan surmised that "Chic Young's strip seems to be assured of survival into a world which will be as alien to it as it already is to McManus's Jiggs." (*The Mechanical Bride*, p. 69)

To McLuhan's great satisfac-
tion, the mind-set that
keeps Dagwood and his
fans alike trapped in a
glass time-capsule is shat-
tered by Al Capp's Li'l Abner.
Capp's satire, irony, and freedom from sentimentality all
work toward the development
of sharpened perception—the

very purpose of McLuhan's own program. The multi-dimen-
sional approach the program requires is

parallelled by the mosaic of
hero images that is Li'l
Abner himself. The real hero
for McLuhan is Capp in his
endless quest to reveal the
delusions and illusions foisted
on society by politicians, business, and the media. McLuhan
made no prediction for the
future of Al Capp's strip, and
unlike Dagwood, Li'l Abner has
not survived, confirming
McLuhan's observation that
society prefers somnambulism to
awareness.

SMILE, IF IT PLEASES YOU, AT THE DEADPAN
DESCRIPTION OF COMIC STRIPS (MCLUHAN CER-
TAINLY WOULDN'T MIND) JUST BEAR IN MIND
THAT NEARLY A DECADE BEFORE ANDY WARHOL
LED THE POP ART REVOLUTION, SHERLOCK
MCLUHAN WAS ALREADY ON THE CASE.

Art
For Our
Sake

The human figures in Bosch paintings react to the chaos and upheaval around them with horror and panic. The same thing is happening today. Panic of a different sort, according to Arthur Kroker, who describes himself as "the Canadian virus" (*Panic Encyclopedia*, p. 265) and "a Canadian successor to McLuhan in many ways, but as a McLuhan for the 1990's." (*Mondo 2000*, #11, 1993, p. 66) In our electronic age, panic is paradoxically both frenzy and inertia. Kroker and his collaborators find the evidence of this ambiguity everywhere from art and advertising to sex and somnambulism, offering updates on the lesson McLuhan taught through the myth of Narcissus.

> *"PANIC ART SITUATES US WITHIN ITS OWN POLAR OPPOSITION: NOSTALGIC DESIRE FOR THE ROCK-SOLID VALUES OF RESPECTABLE MODERNISM VS. HYPER-FAS-CINATION FOR THE VALUELESSNESS OF POSTMODERN OVER-PRODUCTION." (PANIC ENCYCLOPEDIA, P. 19)*

Here frenzy exerts a pull against the inertia and impotence engendered by nostalgia. In other cases, panic is inertia alone, the cancelled identities of figures in the paintings of Alex Colville, Eric Fischl, André Masson, the annihilated image of self that McLuhan and Nevitt refer to, Narcissus moving into the twenty-first century with nineteenth century perceptions. Here it is not a matter of failing to recognize his own image; he is stripped of self-image by yet another new environment.

Panic ads. In *The Mechanical Bride* McLuhan observes that ads for Coca-Cola in the 1950s combine the images of mother and sweetheart, exuding wholesomeness and evoking soft emotions. The subtle religious overtones of this advertising turned absurd when the cover of *Time* (15 May 1950) portrayed the globe sucking a coke. Mom-gal and the coke sucker are long gone, but the soft emotions and soft, universal religion ("I'd like to give the world a Coke, Coke is life") still dominate the advertising.

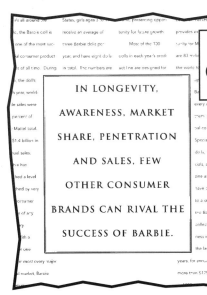

s for wholesomeness, it has been replaced by a hole: "Just draw a picture and put yourself in it. Then make that picture into your transient heaven. Instant Eden. As many Edens as you please. And why even draw your own picture? The pictures are everywhere and each of them has a hole where you can fit." (*Panic Encyclopedia*, p. 54) In the inversion of capitalism created by frenzied publicity, products are not only subordinate to the production of advertising but reduced to the status of fetish— take-out items from the drive-through church. Is Narcissus in the congregation? Yes, and having no problem with recognizing himself:

"WE'VE MADE THE WORLD A MONASTERY WHERE WE WORSHIP OUR SELF-IMAGES." (PANIC ENCYCLOPEDIA, P. 56)

But the panic of frenzy is no less a form of self-amputation than the panic of inertia.

Closure:

The Laws

Of Media

ate in his career, having been repeatedly criticized for failing to provide a scientific basis for his thought, McLuhan reworked his ideas about media and technology in a sequel to *Understanding Media* in collaboration with his son Eric. The new book, titled *Laws of Media: The New Science* (1988), was published eight years after McLuhan's death. In it, McLuhan and Son offer

**FOUR LAWS OF MEDIA,
THE CLAIM THAT THEY HOLD TRUE UNIVERSALLY,
AND
A CHALLENGE TO THE SCIENTIFIC COMMUNITY TO
DISPROVE THEM**

H ow to disprove them? By finding any case where they do not apply or a case which might require a fifth law.

The McLuhans intend their four laws to apply to all media. And to invite the application of these laws to as wide a variety of humankind's endeavors as possible, they offer them not as statements but rather as questions:

The Laws of Media

WHAT DOES IT EXTEND?

WHAT DOES IT MAKE OBSOLETE?

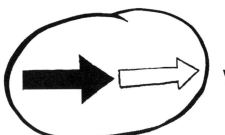
WHAT DOES IT RETRIEVE?

WHAT DOES IT REVERSE INTO?

Remember, these laws are not limited to media of communication; they apply to any artifact, anything of human construction, including language and systems of thought, as we will see below...

Extension ⟹

For "extend," in the phrasing of the first law, we may substitute "enhance," "intensify," "make possible," or "accelerate," depending on the case.

Examples:

❖ A refrigerator enhances the availability of a wide range of foods.

❖ Perspective in drawing and painting intensifies a single point of view.

❖ A photocopier makes possible the reproduction of texts at the speed of the printing press.

❖ The computer accelerates the speed of calculations and retrieval of information.

Obsolescence

Obsolescence is a consequence of extension. When a medium fulfills its function of extending the body or replacing another medium, parts of the environment of whatever was extended become obsolete. For example:

THE REFRIGERATOR MAKES THE ICE MAN'S JOB OBSOLETE.

❖ When the car replaced the horse, it did away with stables, blacksmiths, saddlemakers, harness-menders, hitching posts, horse troughs, carts, and stage-coaches.

Retrieval

Older structures and environments or older forms of action,
human organization, and thought
are revived by the introduction of
a new medium. For example:

❖ A dinner table retrieves
the picking and choosing
options surrendered by
early humans, who discov-
ered in the lap a site for
isolating, manipulating,
and defending their food.

❖ Feminism, in its extremist form, retrieves
the corporate identity of matriarchal society.

Reversal

When a technology is pushed to its limit, as when media are overheated or overextended, it can either take on the opposite of its original features or create the opposite of its intended function. For example:

❖ A dinner table, if very large, no longer offers the ease of reach for which tables were originally designed.

❖ If overcrowded, the dinner table can reverse from a place for sharing food into a site where table mates aggressively intrude on each other's space.

Media Tetrads

TETRADS?

MC WHO?

TETRADS!

I n describing how the laws of media interact, the McLuhans reveal a dynamic pattern of interlocking effects typical of any technology or human construct. In the form of a diagram called a tetrad, the four laws can be shown as follows:

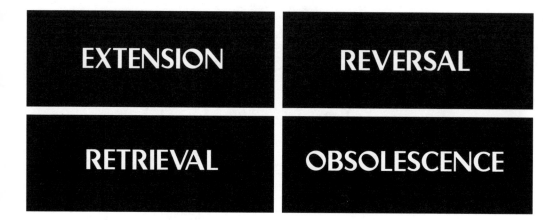

EXTENSION	REVERSAL
RETRIEVAL	OBSOLESCENCE

Extension and obsolescence are linked as action to reaction, which is not the case for retrieval and reversal. A medium does not reverse into its opposite because some older form has been retrieved; rather, it reverses because it is pushed to its limit.

The complementary qualities of these laws can be seen when they are taken in pairs, either horizontally or vertically. Some examples:

Alcohol extends energy but reverses into depression.

The car extends individual privacy but reverses into the corporate privacy of traffic jams.

Earth-orbiting satellites extend the planet and retrieve ecology.

Cubism makes visual space obsolete and reverses into the non-visual.

The microphone makes private space obsolete and reverses into collective space.

Is there a sequence to the laws of media? Obsolescence is a direct and immediate consequence of extension, but one might expect the process of retrieval to take effect only later. For example, with the advent of radio, telegraph wires and connections disappeared almost immediately; the

resulting rekindling of tribal warfare took a little longer. As for reversal, it would seem to set in only when a medium has been in use long enough to have been overextended. All this would suggest that an order imposes itself on the laws of media, but the McLuhans stress that this is not the case:

"[THE] TETRAD OF THE EFFECTS OF TECHNOLOGIES AND ARTIFACTS PRESENTS NOT A SEQUENTIAL PROCESS, BUT RATHER FOUR SIMULTANEOUS ONES. ALL FOUR ASPECTS ARE INHERENT IN EACH ARTIFACT FROM THE START." (P. 99)

There is no "right way to 'read' a tetrad," they note, because "the parts are simultaneous" (p. 129).

A Tetrad Sampler

T he arrangement of the four laws of media relative to each other, as given above, applies to the following examples. They are labelled for the case of WINE but indicated only by the same relative positions for the others. (Don't forget that reversal can be either a reversal of function or a reversal into an opposite form, depending on the case involved; all the examples given below refer to the latter.)

Wine

extends	reverses
grape juice via fermentation	into vinegar

retrieves	makes obsolete
ritual *observance*	common flavours

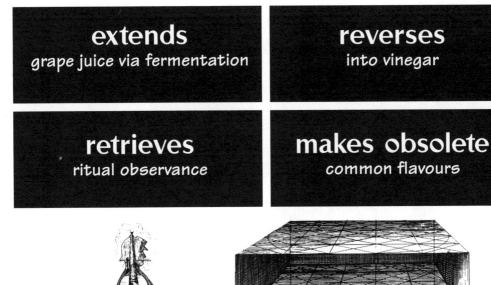

Here's a four-pack of tetrads, straight
from the McLuhans:

Drugs

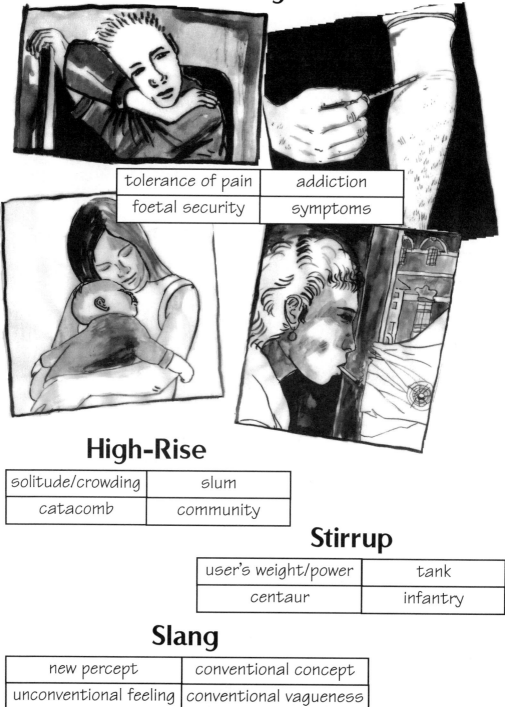

| tolerance of pain | addiction |
| foetal security | symptoms |

High-Rise

| solitude/crowding | slum |
| catacomb | community |

Stirrup

| user's weight/power | tank |
| centaur | infantry |

Slang

| new percept | conventional concept |
| unconventional feeling | conventional vagueness |

Wrapping

It Up

McLuhan glibly dismissed many of his critics in academe as hacks, noting that because they had "been asleep for 500 years," they probably didn't like the idea of anybody coming along and stirring things up. But his critics in the popular media were just as hard-hitting.

Even <u>Wired</u> was less than complimentary of their patron saint, charging that by the time he died, McLuhan was "known in the popular press as an eccentric intellectual whose day in the media spotlight had come and gone".

In October 1979, McLuhan suffered a massive stroke which left him unable to speak. Fifteen months later, in the early morning of New Year's Eve 1980, he died peacefully in his sleep. The inscription on his gravestone, is in digital-analogue typeface and reads:

THE TRUTH SHALL MAKE YOU FREE.

And what, to McLuhan, was truth

He liked to answer that question with a quote from Agatha Christie's criminal sleuth, Hercule Poirot:

"Eet ees whatever upsets zee applecart."

In that regard, McLuhan was a very, very free man, indeed!

If we had to put McLuhan into one sentence, it could be this:

HE ASKS US "WHAT HAVEN'T YOU NOTICED LATELY?"

It's a ridiculous question, but McLuhan wouldn't object. The only reason to ask it is so that we will ASK OURSELVES MORE QUESTIONS.

We can't know WHAT we don't notice unless we ask ourselves WHY we don't notice more about our world. And this is where McLuhan's teachings about media and environments come in. McLuhan doesn't care if we ask different questions and come up with different answers than he did, as long as we discover something about our world and what is happening to it.

McLuhan published hundreds of articles and over a dozen books. Here are all the book titles and a selection of the articles.

Books

The Mechanical Bride: Folklore of Industrial Man. New York, 1951; London, 1967.

The Gutenberg Galaxy: The Making of Typographic Man. Toronto, 1962.

Understanding Media: The Extensions of Man. New York and London, 1964. Translated into French by Jean Paré and published as *Pour comprendre les média: les prolongements technologiques de l'homme.* Montreal, 1972. English edition of 1964 reprinted by MIT Press, 1995.

Explorations in Communication: An Anthology. (edited by Edmund Carpenter and Marshall McLuhan) Boston, 1966. (second printing)

The Medium is the Massage: An Inventory of Effects. (with Quentin Fiore) New York, 1967.

Verbi-Voco-Visual Explorations. New York, 1967. (Reprint of Explorations, no. 8)

Through the Vanishing Point: Space in Poetry and Painting. (with Harley Parker) New York: 1968.

War and Peace in the Global Village; an inventory of some of the current spastic situations that could be eliminated by more feedforward. (with Quentin Fiore) New York, 1968. Translated into French as *Guerre et paix dans le village planétaire; un inventaire de quelques situations spasmodiques courantes qui pourraient être supprimées par le feedforward.* Paris, 1970.

The Interior Landscape: The Literary Criticism of Marshall McLuhan, 1943-1962. (edited by Eugene McNamara) New York, 1969.

Counterblast. Toronto, 1969.

Culture Is Our Business. New York, 1970.

From Cliché to Archetype. (with Wilfred Watson) New York, 1970.

Voices of Literature: Sounds, Masks, Roles. (with R. J. Schoeck) New York, 1971.

Take Today: The Executive as Dropout. (with Barrington Nevitt) Toronto, 1972.

City as Classroom: Understanding Language and Media. (with Eric McLuhan and Kathryn Hutchon) Toronto, 1977.

Letters of Marshall McLuhan. (selected and edited by Matie Molinaro, Corinne McLuhan, and William Toye) Toronto, 1987.

Laws of Media: The New Science. (with Eric McLuhan) Toronto, 1988.

The Global Village: transformations in world life and media in the 21st century. (with Bruce R. Powers) New York, 1989.

Essential McLuhan. (edited by Eric McLuhan & Frank Zingrone) Toronto, 1995.

Articles

G. K. Chesterton: A Practical Mystic. *The Dalhousie Review* 15 (1936), 455-464.

Poetic vs. Rhetorical Exegesis: The Case for Leavis Against Richards and Empson. *The Sewanee Review* 52 (1944), 266-76.

American Advertising. *Horizon* 93 (October 1947), 132-41.

Joyce, Aquinas, and the Poetic Process. *Renascence* 4 (1951), 3-11.

Defrosting Canadian Culture. *American Mercury* 74 (March 1952), 91-7.

Technology and Political Change. *International Journal* 7 (Summer 1952), 189-95.

Culture without Literacy. *Explorations: Studies in Culture and Communication* 1 (December 1953), 117-27.

Media as Art Forms. *Explorations: Studies in Culture and Communication* 2 (April 1954), 6-13.

Sight, Sound, and the Fury. *Commonweal* 60 (1954), 168-197. Reprinted in Bernard Rosenberg and David Manning White, eds., *Mass Culture: The Popular Arts in America*. London, 1957, pp. 489-495.

The ABCED-minded. *Explorations: Studies in Culture and Communication* 5 (June 1955), 12-18.

Myth and Mass Media. *Daedalus* 88 (1959), 339-48.

Effects of the Improvements of Communication Media. *The Journal of Economic History* 20 (December 1960), 566-75.

The Medium is the Message. *Forum* (University of Houston), Summer 1960, 19-24.

The All-at-Once World of Marshall McLuhan. *Vogue*, August 1966, 70-73, 111.

A Dialogue: Q. & A. In Gerald E. Stearn, ed., *McLuhan: Hot and Cool: A Primer for the Understanding of and a Critical Symposium* with a *Rebuttal* by McLuhan. New York, 1967, pp. 260-92.

A Candid Conversation with the High Priest of Popcult and Metaphysician of Media. *Playboy*, March 1969, 53-74, 158.

Understanding McLuhan—and fie on any who don't. *The Globe and Mail*, 10 September 1973, p. 7.

McLuhan's Laws of the Media. *Technology and Culture*, January 1975, 74-78.

Other Works Quoted From

KROKER, Arthur, Marilouise Kroker, and David Cook, with others. *Panic Encyclopedia*. Montreal, 1989.

MONDO 200, #11, 1993, p66.

STEARN, Gerald Emanuel. *McLuhan: Hot and Cool. A Primer for the Understanding of and a Critical Symposium with a Rebuttal by McLuhan.* New York, 1967.

WRIGHT, F. A., ed. *Lemprière's Classical Dictionary of Proper Names mentioned in Ancient Authors.* London, 1958.

Other Works Not Quoted From

DE KERCKHOVE, Derrick. *The Skin of Culture: Investigating the New Electronic Reality.* Toronto, 1995.

KROKER, Arthur. *Technology and the Canadian Mind: Innis/ McLuhan/Grant.* Montreal, 1984.

MARCHAND, Philip. *Marshall McLuhan: The Medium and the Messenger.* Toronto, 1989.

MILLER, Jonathan. *McLuhan.* London, 1971.

NEVITT, Barrington, and Maurice McLuhan, eds. *Who Was Marshall McLuhan?* Toronto, 1995.

POWE, B. W. *Outage: A Journey into Electric City.* Toronto, 1995.

SANDERSON, George, and Frank Macdonald, eds. *Marshall McLuhan: The Man and His Message.* Golden, Colorado, 1989.

AND HERE'S SOMETHING FOR YOU NET-SURFERS!!
Check out McLUHAN STUDIES:
http://www.icgc.com/mcluhan_studies/

index

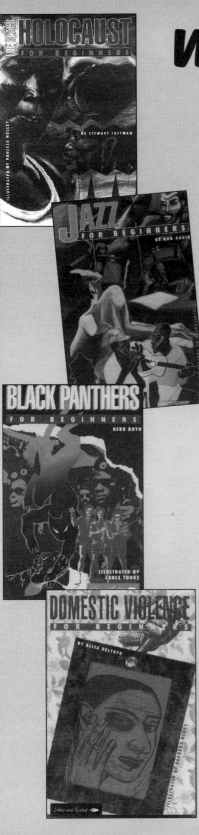

WHAT'S NEW?

THE BLACK HOLOCAUST FOR BEGINNERS

By S.E. Anderson; Illustrated by the Cro-maat Collective and Vanessa Holley

The Black Holocaust, a travesty that killed no less than 50 million African human beings, is the most underreported major event in world history. But it won't be for long. *The Black Holocaust For Beginners* — part indisputably documented chronicle, part passionately engaging narrative, will put this tragic event in plain sight where it belongs!
Trade paper, $11.00 ($15.75 Can., £6.99 UK), ISBN 0-86316-178-2

JAZZ FOR BEGINNERS

By Ron David; Illustrated by Vanessa Holley

An amazingly thorough guide to Jazz that is as full of blood, guts and humor as the music it describes.
Trade paper, $11.00 ($15.75 Can., £6.99 UK), ISBN 0-86316-165-0

BLACK PANTHERS FOR BEGINNERS

By Herb Boyd; Illustrated by Lance Tooks

The late 1960s, when the Panthers captured the imagination of the nation's youth, was a time of revolution. While their furious passage was marked by death, destruction, and government sabotage, the Panthers left an instructive legacy for anyone who dares to challenge the system. But don't settle for half-truths or fictionalized accounts. Learn the whole story, the way it really happened, by American Book Award winner Herb Boyd.
Trade paper, $11.00 ($15.75 Can., £6.99 UK), ISBN 0-86316-196-0

DOMESTIC VIOLENCE FOR BEGINNERS

By Alisa Del Tufo; Illustrated by Barbara Henry

Why do men hurt women — and why has so little been done about it? What can be done? A no-holds barred look at the causes and effects of spousal abuse — an epidemic by any standards that is still ignored. This book is not a luxury; it should be part of a survival kit given to everyone who buys a Marriage License. Your life — or your child's life — could depend on it.
Trade paper, $11.00 ($15.75 Can., £6.99 UK), ISBN 0-86316-1173-1

Writers and Readers

WRITERS AND READERS PUBLISHING, INC.
625 Broadway, New York, NY 10012

To order, or for a free catalog, please call (212) 982-3158; fax (212) 777-4924. MC/Visa accepted.

149

SUBSTITUTE!

And knowledge, as you will discover in our "Documentary Comic Books," is fun! Each book is painstakingly researched, humorously written and illustrated in whatever style best suits the subject at hand.

MAKING
COMPLEX SUBJECTS
SIMPLE
AND
SERIOUS SUBJECTS
FUN!!!

Chomsky For Beginners

by David Cogswell; illustrated by Paul Gordon

Race For Beginners

by S.E. Anderson Illustrated by The Cro-Maat Collective

McLuhan For Beginners

by W. Terrence Gordon; illustrated by Susan Willmarth

I-Ching For Beginners

by Brandon Toropov; illustrated by John Kane

The History of Eastern Europe For Beginners

by Beck, Mast and Tapper

That's **Writers and Readers**, where *For Beginners*™ books began! Remember, if it doesn't say...

Writers and Readers

... it's not an <u>original</u> *For Beginners* ™ book!

HOW TO GET GREAT THINKERS TO COME TO YOUR HOME...

To order any current titles of Writers and Readers **For Beginners**™ books, please fill out the coupon below and enclose a check made out to **Writers and Readers Publishing, Inc.** To order by phone (with Master Card or Visa), or to receive a <u>free</u> <u>catalog</u> of all our **For Beginners**™ books, please call (212) 982-3158.

Price per book: $11.00

Individual Order Form   (clip out or copy complete page)

Book Title	Quantity	Amount
	Sub Total:	
N.Y. residents add 8 1/4% sales tax		
Shipping & Handling ($3.00 for the first book; $.60 for each additional book)		
	TOTAL	

Name _____

Address _____

City _____ State _____ Zip Code _____

Phone number (___) _____

MC / VISA (circle one)   Account # _____ Expires _____

Send check or money order to: **Writers and Readers Publishing**, P.O. Box 461 Village Station, New York, NY 10014 (212) 982-3158, fx (212) 777-4924; In the U.K: **Airlift Book Company**, 8, The Arena, Mollison Ave., Enfield, EN3 7NJ, England 0181.804.0044. Or contact us for a <u>FREE</u> <u>CATALOG</u> of all our *For Beginners*™ titles.

Addiction & Recovery ($11.0)
African History ($9.95)
Arabs & Israel ($12.00)
Architecture ($11.00)
Babies ($9.95)
Biology ($11.00)
Black History ($9.95)
Black Holocaust ($11.00)
Black Panthers ($11.00)
Black Women ($9.95)
Brecht ($9.95)
Classical Music ($9.95)
Computers ($11.00)
DNA ($9.95)
Domestic Violence ($11.0)
Elvis ($6.95)
Erotica ($7.95)
Food ($7.95)
Foucault ($9.95)
Freud ($9.95)
Health Care ($9.95)
Heidegger ($9.95)
Hemingway ($9.95)
History of Clowns ($11.00)
Ireland ($9.95)
Islam ($9.95)
Jazz ($11.00)
Jewish Holocaust ($11.00)
J.F.K. ($9.95)
Judaism ($9.95)
Kierkegaard ($11.00)
Malcolm X ($9.95)
Mao ($9.95)
Martial Arts ($11.00)
Miles Davis ($9.00)
Nietzsche ($9.95)
Opera ($11.00)
Orwell ($4.95)
Pan-Africanism ($9.95)
Philosophy ($11.00)
Plato ($11.00)
Psychiatry ($9.95)
Rainforests ($7.95)
Sartre ($11.00)
Saussure ($11.00)
Sex ($9.95)
UNICEF ($11.00)
United Nations ($11.00)
World War II ($8.95)
Zen ($11.00)